Tales of Two Coyotes

adventures with power animals

Stella Longland

a Cave of Clay book

Copyright © Stella Longland 2018

Cover design by Stella Longland ©

second edition 2018
re-titled and with text revisions

All rights reserved. No part of this publication may be reproduced, stored in a retrieval system, or transmitted in any form or by any means without prior written permission of the copyright owner. Nor can it be circulated in any form of binding or cover other than that in which it is published and without similar condition including this condition being imposed on a subsequent purchaser.

(first edition 2010 copyright © Stella Longland 2010
title: Tall Tales & Short Stories)

British Library Cataloguing in Publication Data
A catalogue record for this book is available from the British Library

ISBN 978-1-9999024-0-7

contact the author: stella@peacechamber.co.uk
related websites: www.peacechamber.co.uk
www.somethingdoeshappen.co.uk

Dedication

To My Teacher

These journeys were taken under the guidance of
my Teacher, Alexander,
over three years, during seminars that I attended,
many of them under the auspices of
the Findhorn Foundation.
He would give us instructions before each journey
and generally he would play the drum
to mark the travelling time.
Occasionally we travelled to music,
and I have indicated the journeys
that were taken in this way.

Thank you, Alexander, for being instrumental
in unlocking and opening my mind.

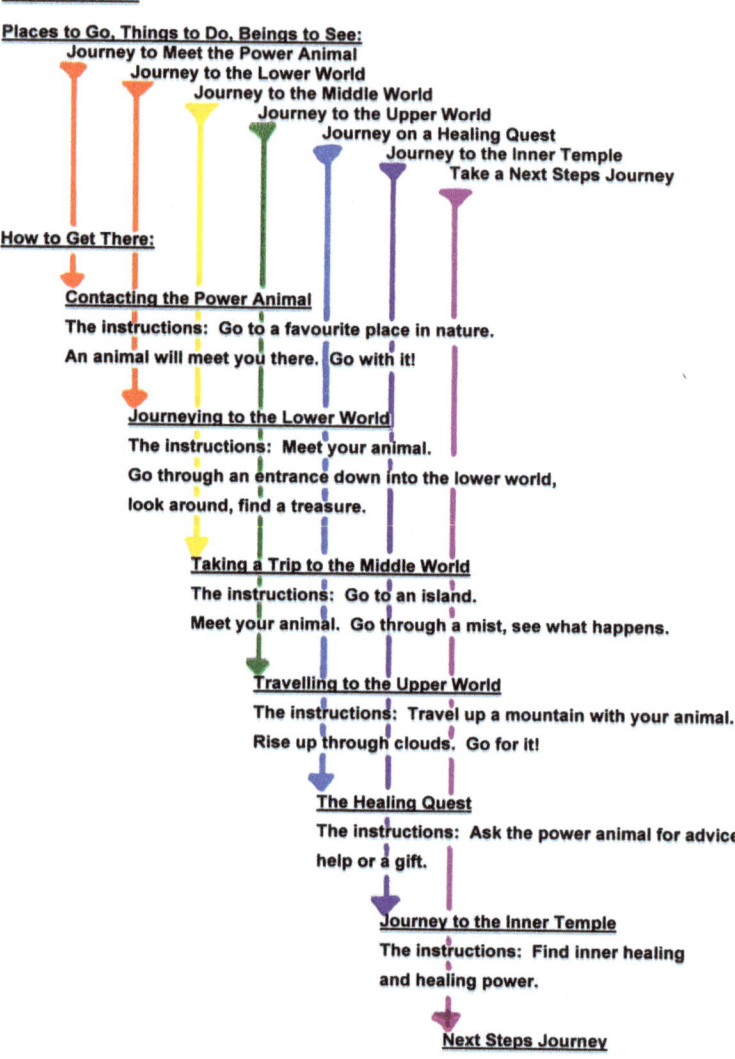

Coyote Dreams:

Places to Go, Things to Do, Beings to See:
Journey to Meet the Power Animal
Journey to the Lower World
Journey to the Middle World
Journey to the Upper World
Journey on a Healing Quest
Journey to the Inner Temple
Take a Next Steps Journey

How to Get There:

Contacting the Power Animal
The instructions: Go to a favourite place in nature.
An animal will meet you there. Go with it!

Journeying to the Lower World
The instructions: Meet your animal.
Go through an entrance down into the lower world,
look around, find a treasure.

Taking a Trip to the Middle World
The instructions: Go to an island.
Meet your animal. Go through a mist, see what happens.

Travelling to the Upper World
The instructions: Travel up a mountain with your animal.
Rise up through clouds. Go for it!

The Healing Quest
The instructions: Ask the power animal for advice,
help or a gift.

Journey to the Inner Temple
The instructions: Find inner healing
and healing power.

Next Steps Journey
The instructions: Use your
imagination!

<u>Consult the final 5 pages to find</u>
  About the Author
  About this Book
  About the Travelling Technique
  Other Books by the Author
  Contents index

ONE

Crashing through Fire

Burnt Out

The Metal Man

Roads are Measured in Feet

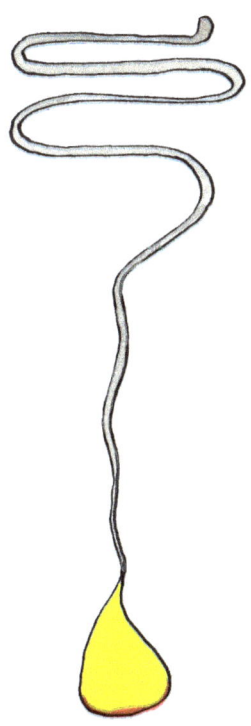

Contacting the Power Animal
Go to a favourite place in nature.
An animal will meet you there. Go with it!

1. Crashing through Fire

As usual, I was panicking well ahead before the journey had even started. While giving the instructions Alexander said: "I suggest you go to some familiar and favourite place in nature." Immediately I was thinking: "Where? Where shall I go? What will happen?" Oh, how I would like to be able to wait patiently and not try to see the end before the beginning.

In the event I did not choose a place I had visited in this world; I chose instead a place I had visited several times in meditations. I decided that I would go to the clearing in the forest where someone had lit a small fire deep in a pile of brown leaves. The air in the forest was still. The scene was autumnal. A thin curl of smoke rose straight up from the leaf pile and deep within the fire glowed. I knew I could wait there and eventually someone would come.

The drumming started and I realized with shock that I was approaching this special place at high speed. Flying through the air and out of control, I crashed into the leaf pile and right through the fire. On the other side there was a wolf-like creature waiting for me. Wolf-like? Well, it looked pretty wolfish to me. It was jet black, it was very skinny, and it had a very long, narrow face. No sooner had I arrived, than it turned away and set off into the darkness. I grabbed the disappearing tail and hung on in order to be able to follow. We were moving fast; there did not seem to be any obstacles in our path, but it got darker, and darker, and darker, until it was completely pitch dark.

We came to a halt and I heard the wolfish creature say: "Here we are!" In an exasperated tone, I enquired: "Where?" Clearly, we needed light. Unclenching my fist, I opened up my right hand; in the bowl of my palm a small flame flickered. Briefly wondering if it came from the crashed-through fire, I held it up so that we could see where we were. Perhaps the creature could see in the dark, but I couldn't.

The black creature started dancing and I followed suit. The tiny flame became a bonfire and, as we danced around it, the light increased and the space got larger and larger as if, by dancing, we were busy hollowing out a cave in the darkness. I could see that the walls and floor were smooth and brown, like beaten earth, and as we danced our shadows flickered up and down around us, so that it seemed as if there were many Beings in there, not just we two.

Becoming still, I found myself standing in the great space that we had made. A snake had coiled itself around me and I began to grow until I was slowly pushing my way up through the ground above the cave. I was becoming a tree. But this tree was growing in a strange way; a fully-grown tree was coming up, not a seed germinating to become a sapling but a mature trunk thrusting its way through the ground. It was my perception that the trunk, which was pushing its way through the ground, belonged to an enormous pine tree. This transformation was the most difficult part of the journey and I put all my energy into it in order to succeed.

Once through the ground I rose up and floated, my consciousness suspended somewhere near the top of the trunk, held there by some force that felt like the force between similarly charged poles in two magnets. Not the force of attraction where the opposite poles rush together, but the other force where like poles push apart. Suspended in this way in the great pine tree I felt completely peaceful. I felt that I would be happy to be there for some considerable time but not for ever, no, not for forever. I noticed that the skittish black creature was knocking around at the base of the tree, doing canine things. I was interested in those things.

The drum beat changed and I was being called back. I came back, down into the underground chamber and back through the darkness. I was reluctant to leave the tree quite so soon. Yes, I felt regret, but I came back.

<u>Journeying to the Lower World</u>
Meet your animal. Go through an entrance down
into the lower world, look around, find a treasure.

2. Burnt Out

When the drumming started, I unexpectedly developed a terrible tickle in my throat. I badly wanted to cough. I felt as if I was getting a sudden cold, was going to lose my voice, and wouldn't be able to speak or sing for the rest of the seminar. The tickling throat was overwhelming and threatening to destroy the whole trip, but I managed to wrench my attention away from this area of my body and the tickling abruptly stopped.

I tried to find the site of the fire that I had, accidentally, destroyed the day before. I did find a fire-ish sort-of-a-thing, but it was more like a bulb. I mean the bulb of a plant, not a light bulb. It was a strange mixture of fire, flower and bulb. The black creature was there and, again, it set off the moment it saw me. I shouted: "Hey, hey, come here. I want to greet you." So it came and, standing on its hind legs, put its front paws on my shoulders and licked my face. It was indeed a queer creature, skittish, thin, too light, too small, to be a wolf. I said: "Take me somewhere different." It said: "Well, be prepared not to be able to make any sense of it, or remember anything of it when you come back." I thought I could agree to this. I had already journeyed to several places that it was incredibly difficult to make any sense of, so I thought I could take another one. I nodded agreement and we set off. But immediately we started travelling, I realized that I wasn't prepared. I wanted to understand everything and I definitely wanted to be able to bring something back.

Then the whole journey became a struggle. We went down into the ground through a curious semi-circular opening lying flat on the earth. Its edges were too smooth and too regular to be part of the natural world; it was like an open manhole, like the entrance to a drain with the cover taken off. Straightaway I was rejecting it as an inappropriate part of a journey to the lower world and trying to remember it at the same time.

Once through this entrance, the first things I saw were spiky and black. The impression was of dark black spikes against a slightly lighter background. I realized that they were bare branches silhouetted against a dusky sky; we had come into a burnt out forest, completely burnt out. It occurred to me that by crashing through the fire yesterday I might have set the forest ablaze. I decided not to dwell on that possibility, saying to myself: "No! This isn't right. I don't want this. I can't bear this. I don't want my lower world to be a charred forest. I won't have it." I tried to move on, but it just didn't work out. I tried a change of form, and I became a yellow creature, a yellow creature of the same species as the black one so that we made a pair. That was a brief solace, but I couldn't make anything last.

Eventually, obviously fed up of me, my travelling companion said: "Come and rest here with me. Come, let's rest at the side of this burnt out tree." So we curled up together by the trunk of the fallen tree, at the point where the main body split into branches. Out of the corner of my restless eye, I thought I saw some flashes of green. Immediately my mind began to race: "I'm going to re-grow this forest. I'm a yellow-golden colour, like the sun, so I can re-grow it." But the green vanished, and the restless torment went on and on. I couldn't lie there. I couldn't lie still and be quiet. Twitching and fidgeting, constantly on the move, I tossed and turned.

The situation was impossible and eventually, I think in desperation, the creature turned us both into a piece of jewellery. On this piece of jewellery, we were two dogs standing on our hind legs opposite each other. To my mind, the two dogs looked like Anubis and Set, power animals from Khemet, the Black Land: the name of Egypt for the ancient inhabitants. The black one was, of course, Anubis, which meant that the yellow one was Set. That was a bit of a problem to me: Set was the destroyer. The yellow creature was the personification of all destructiveness and I was the yellow creature. I couldn't come to terms with the implications of that, but through the mental turmoil came thoughts of an ancient temple sanctuary in Khemet, a place of silence, stillness and peace.

Suddenly I noticed that I was becoming a black stone statue; as a last resort, I had been turned into a statue to calm me down. I became very calm. My mind became as smooth and still as the stone. My mind and body were stone and only my visionary eyes could move. Looking up, I saw that the top of my head was splitting open and a V-shaped opening with sides that bowed towards each other was forming there.

Looking through the gap made by this V, I began to see a landscape, but I couldn't make any sense of it. There seemed to be grey and white creatures moving there. I saw abstract shapes representing muscles and flanks; they were grazing animals by the look of them. And there was green, the colour of green that I associate with grass. I didn't see a scene of animals grazing in a field; I interpreted something incomprehensible into that. And, as this landscape opened up, I heard myself say with deep gratitude: "Thank you, Coyote! Thank you, Coyote!"

Now, even as a statue, I could still think, but the thinking was of a different kind. It was perceiving something not of my world and trying to make sense of it for my world. In the burnt out forest the thinking I had been engaged in was the opposite. It was the thinking of expectation, logical thinking based on the known, unable to see the unknown or even to acknowledge it. As I lay now, perceiving statuesquely, I was full of gratitude that I had reached that quiet state, but also shocked that my liberated psyche had so clearly acknowledged the Coyote. It was true then that the Coyote was attached to me.

I was way, way, out when the drum beat changed, but I was whizzed effortlessly back by the Coyote, floating on a yellow ribbon of light, and at the end I wanted again to say thanks: "Thank you, Coyote! Thank you, Coyote, for helping me."

> Taking a Trip to the Middle World
> Go to an island. Meet your animal.
> Go through a mist, see what happens.

3. The Metal Man

I stood on the bank looking out over the water and I wondered: "How am I going to get to the island?" Then I noticed that there was a line of large, flat stepping-stones. It was, however, quite a long walk over these stones to the island. I began, stepping across them meaningfully, but I soon got bored so I started to jump, skip, hop and roll over. In this way, I arrived at the island.

The air was clear at the place where I stepped onto the shore, but a few steps inland there was a bank of fog. I walked in feeling a little panicky; the visibility reduced as the mist closed in around me. I felt its cold touch on my arms. I looked down and saw the mist condensing around me forming a yellow cloak. Immediately

I thought: "Oh, here is the Coyote." And we stepped out into a landscape of green grass. We were standing in a hollow and all around us the ground rose, forming hillocks and hummocks. The air was calm and clear.

Then there began a mental tussle as I panicked that the journey was not going to move on. Eventually the sandy-yellow Coyote said to me: "Just sit down on the grass and take some healing, for goodness sake!" So I sat down, looked at the grass, and thought about things that I had done earlier in the day.

When I looked up a pale-golden Metal Man was standing there. I felt very confused: "Where has he appeared from?" Actually, he looked more like a robot than a man, and I wondered if the Coyote had made a robot, but, no, I think the golden man had walked down the incline from the left to stand with us in the hollow. I thought: "This is very weird." But then I recognized the golden substance that he seemed to be made of, as being similar to something I had seen in a meditation some months before and I began to feel more hopeful.

Although the landscape was still fully there in my mind, I became very aware of my body lying in the seminar room and the two realms began to interact with each other. The metal began to flow into my supine body. It pulsed in through the soles of my feet and began to move up my legs. When it got to my knees, I noticed that I was beginning to look very similar to the metal Being who was standing next to the Coyote. I looked strangely peculiar; something about my body shape had changed, as if all my ins were smoothed outs. Something about the feel of my body had changed, as if I was all of one substance and did not have sinews and bones. It was like wearing a golden suit only the gold went right through my body and all of my body was gold.

I tried to keep very calm and not reject or be surprised by anything that was happening. The physical sensation was very pleasant and very unusual, not possible to describe, only to feel. The smooth golden metal moved on up and the feeling got very intense at my belly. Then it moved upwards again. When it got to my heart it began to move in waves so that it behaved even more like a fluid than a metal, but I would still describe it as metallic, well, I don't know: it was a strange substance. It carried on from my heart and began to move into my arms. I felt it very strongly then; it flowed right down my fingers, circling round in the fingertips. Then it moved up to my head, here it moved more slowly, in many thin lines. It seemed to encounter blockages, but it kept moving in, moving in.

The numinous Metal Man was pouring more golden light into the cauldron, which was my heart, saying: "Take in as much as you can. Take in as much as you can. Take in as much as you can." Till it reached a point where the movement stopped, as if triggered by this, a chasm opened in the centre of my body, which ran from the base of my pelvis to the top of my abdomen. The movement began again and the golden fluid flowed into this chasm, pouring in over the sides in a shimmering cascade. As I watched it flood over the edge, I noticed that it was carrying the golden coyote-essence in its current. I held my breath. I saw the fluid body of the Coyote go swiftly over the side in the golden stream and I was able to look in and see worlds upon worlds, worlds everywhere. I didn't know my body had all these worlds, but I looked into the chasm and it went down vastly, vastly, amazingly. It went down and also spread out sideways, huge and forever.

After some moments of awe, I thought: "Where is the Coyote now? I'm supposed to be travelling with the Coyote and not forgetting about him." So I called: "Coyote, where are you?" He replied: "You'll have to find me." It was like a game of hide-and-seek and I looked everywhere. This had been a journey through my body and so I walked my awareness all over my body, but I couldn't see him. It was like there wasn't anywhere in the universe for him to be except my body which, I had discovered, was the universe, but I couldn't see him anywhere.

Now the only place that I couldn't see was at the back of me, between my shoulder blades, so I said: "You are there. You must be there." I was right. He came round to the front from the left side and sat on my breastbone, just below the collarbones. He was very small, the height of the first joint of my thumb. Sitting on his haunches, looking at me, he said: "It doesn't matter how small I am, I've still got the power!" He sat there motionless for a while as if to let that remark sink in: "It doesn't matter how small I am ...."

Then something seemed to say: "You'd better start to go back because it is going to take a long time to consolidate all this in your memory and to go back through all the states, so go; even though the return drumming hasn't started, go!" You see, I have discovered that I can't use my memory as I travel out on these journeys because that memory is based on the way things usually work and so it gets very intrusive and judgemental and destroys the journey. The only way I can remember is on the way back, when it has all already happened, by going slowly through the journey backwards with the Coyote and he helps me fix it in my memory as I go. So I went back through it, back, back through it all, to the stage where my body was lying there, before the gold substance started to flow in.

At that point I thought again of the earlier experience where I first saw this metal and I journeyed again; I journeyed away backwards in time now, back to that place and recaptured the experience. I was standing on a golden metal floor, which was covered with geometric patterns and stretched to the horizon. A liquid golden sun, surrounded by rays like petals with rounded tips, was rising. I stayed there, enjoying seeing that beautiful scene again, until I thought: "Wait, this isn't the beginning of today's journey. I'd better go from here now. I'd better start going backwards, or is it forwards now?"

I travelled again and I came to the mist. Here I took off the mist-made cloak and laid it on the ground, saying: "Thank you, Coyote, for that great gift of a travelling coat." I walked through the mist and crossed the stepping-stones to the regular beat of the drum, walking much more calmly than I had done when I initially came across. On reaching the mainland, I condensed my consciousness back into my body and I let the sound of the drum come in and vibrate all up and down my physical body, a great feeling. Then, very shortly after that, the drum beat quickened and called us back.

Travelling to the Upper World
Travel up a mountain with your animal.
Rise up through clouds. Go for it!

4. Roads are Measured in Feet

I wondered what I would like from this journey. I decided that I would like to be better attuned to the spirit world. Yes, I would like to be tuned in.

The drumming started and I found myself in a rolling landscape looking back at Alexander, who seemed to be standing some distance away, beating the drum and watching me set off. I was laughing and thinking: "You ....! You made this as difficult as possible. You encouraged a ramshackle mess, threw us from intensity to triviality and back again, switched from the mysterious to the mundane without drawing breath. Yes, revelled in chaos!"

I turned round and there in front of me was a yellow road. "Hello, Coyote. Tell me, how am I going to get the other members of the group to accept that you are a road?" He replied: "Well, roads are measured in feet, you know." That seemed logical, he had four of them, and so I started walking along the road up a slight incline.

Suddenly the road took off like a jet plane and I found myself climbing into the sky on its back. In front of me, I could see the head of the Coyote. I reached forward and clung onto his neck, feeling the terrific acceleration as we went up through the clouds, hurtled through the atmosphere, and arrived in space.

Space struck me as rather empty and I thought: "What are we going to do here?" The Coyote suggested: "I'll make a rug for you to lie on." And he made himself into a finely woven camel coloured rug with wide-spaced long twisted fringes hanging down at each end. I lay upon it. It was soft, lovely. I felt very relaxed. I lay on my back and looked at the stars; millions of silver points in jet black space stretching away for ever. With deep satisfaction, I thought: "Good, this is great. I love this Coyote. I'll just lie here and I'll receive messages and re-attunement from the spirit world. I am perfectly prepared, great!" I dangled my hands over the sides of the rug and felt its soft texture, sensing the miles and miles below me to the

Earth and feeling intensely the quiet, still, cool and refreshing clarity of space.

Suddenly a bushy golden-yellow tail came up from below and flopped over my left leg. I thought: "Oh, don't start messing about now!" Immediately the blanket started to undulate. Then it rolled up, with me inside it, and raced through the sky. It accelerated upwards, spun downwards, flipped and twisted. My head was poking out of the end and I was trying desperately to keep my eyes open to see what was going on. I quickly checked my physical body. I could feel my eyes doing rapid eye movements all over the place so I knew it was really going on, and I was being rolled and raced through space. I was getting dizzy. "Oh no, surely I haven't got to go into a dizzy spin?" I shouted at the Coyote: "You've never taken me anywhere! Just take me out, don't take me in!" The Coyote shouted back, like a hysterical sergeant major: "Evacuate! Evacuate!" I knew that I had to stop getting sick from rolling with the roll and flowing with the flow. To achieve this I centred my concentration. I shrunk my concentration into a tiny, tight, round capsule of pulsating magenta-red in the middle of all this rolling chaos.

That worked, everything calmed down, and the Coyote said calmly: "Stand outside your mind." As he said that I felt the power come into my feet and rise up to my knees and I thought: "Oh good, I've reached some state where the power can come in." And I lay there open for the power to come in. Slowly it came up my body. Then the Coyote said again, with urgency: "Stand outside your mind! Stand outside your mind!" Somehow, in some way, I moved to the right and felt a subtle change. I thought with surprise: "Now I can think about anything. It doesn't make any difference now because a process has started and is ongoing." It was like when I once woke up in the middle of the night and found that healing was pouring through me into my partner lying next to me and I just thought: "Nothing to do with me," and went back to sleep. I felt liberated then. I felt liberated now, so free that I was able to go back through the journey so far and fix it in my memory without jeopardizing what was happening.

Then, behind the drumming, I heard a sound from outside the room. I was aware of the inner journey and the outside world at the same time, and the two were interwoven. It sounded like a garbage wagon. I thought about the spiritual healing session the seminar group did the night before. When I had been lying down after receiving healing I heard a voice saying: "Throw this body on the garbage. Throw this body out with the garbage." It was speaking to me about my physical body and I found it rather an amusing idea. What would the person who had just channelled healing to me have thought if they had also heard it?

I was aware of excited voices calling out within my mind: "The frontal renovations are finished." Intrigued, I walked into the front of my head and there were two marvellous new bay windows. I realized that my house was being reconstructed; my house was being rebuilt. The front room was spacious, although the ceiling was low, and through the two new windows I could see the bright sky. I suspected that my house was on a cliff and that it looked out over the sea, but I was admiring the windows from the door of the room, like a house buyer with an estate agent at their shoulder, and I only guessed this.

There was some more clanking outside the seminar room. It sounded like scaffolding being put up and, indeed, inside my mind there was incredible activity, builders were busy everywhere. The Coyote took me to the central staircase, which was the pituitary gland, and he said: "This is the staircase to the upper levels, but we haven't built them yet." He continued, even more enthusiastically: "Come and look at the extension out the back though; we've made these great rooms out the back." We went to the back where there were steps going down to a cellar. I heard some more clanking outside. It sounded like beer barrels rolling down into the cellar of a pub and I said loudly, in horror: "I don't want to live in a pub." Then I whined self pityingly: "I don't want to live in a pub." The

Coyote said: "Ah, don't worry, there's another level down below this. Come down this staircase here. We've built massive rooms down here." I went down there and I appreciated light, even though these cellars were two floors down, I felt the presence of light. I looked out and saw a huge landscape. He said: "There's loads of room for extensions down here. And, the best thing is, you don't need planning permission because they're underground."

    I was in the cellar looking at the light, and he was telling me about the planning potential, when the drum beat changed and I had to come back fast. Because the journey had been so intense, so different, so trippy, as I went swiftly back through all the stages I felt that the chances of me losing it were immense. When the rapid drumming ended I lay on the seminar room floor, half in and half out my body, and, oh, I was in a radically altered state for what seemed like forever. Luckily, the others were busy writing down their stories and so it didn't matter. I daren't move, couldn't move, in case it all vanished, I just lay there going through the story. I went slowly and intensely back, backwards, then forward, forwards, again.

    This mind that was no longer in my mind, yes, in my new house, my bungalow, well, they were still building it. It was total chaos basically. It seemed like chaos. The rooms that were finished were fantastic, but there was plenty that was unfinished. During the trip I had laughed and laughed; it was all so funny. I am sure it was a detached bungalow because, certainly, my attitude was very detached. Anyway, backwards, forwards, backwards, forwards: fix, fix, fix, fix. Eventually I managed to get myself back, memory intact, but for a time I thought, you know, these radical structural alterations were going to be too much for me and I wouldn't get back here.

TWO

Safe in the Sky

Green Eyes

Live Lightly

The Fall

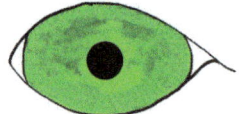 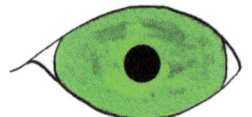

<u>Contacting the Power Animal</u>
Go to a favourite place in nature.
An animal will meet you there. Go with it!

5. Safe in the Sky

I chose to go to a marvellous tree that I know. I found it in the winter on a still frosty day of brilliant sunshine. I didn't know what sort of tree it was, but it was a beautiful shape. The trunk was straight and broad to a height of eight feet; above that the branches, growing out from the central trunk at shallow angles, spread wider and wider forming a large circle in the high canopy of the wood and creating a similar clear circular space on the ground below. In the uppermost branches there was a squirrels' nest. I sat and watched five grey squirrels romping through the branches and racing up and down the trunk, bounding into the adjacent trees in a rush of january joy.

Next time I visited the tree was in full flower. The lower branches were bare; the upper branches that could reach the light were a mass of pink blossom, a glorious, glorious sight. The air was full of the sound of bees and other insects indulging in a pollen frenzy. I could tell, from the flowers and the emerging leaves, what type of tree it was: an apple tree. A forty-foot high wild apple tree, but I could hardly believe an apple tree could grow that big; it must be ancient.

So that is where I went. I stood there for a long time watching the squirrels. Then I noticed the Coyote to my left. I felt lucky because recently he has been enjoying himself, as a card shark, gambling on a Mississippi riverboat. He's been busy playing pontoon, shouting: "Twist or stick? Anyone who sticks is stuck!" I felt lucky he'd got the time to visit. He looked at the squirrels leaping around and he said: "This is fun! Let's hunt one. How are we going to get up there?"

The ground began to shake and I thought: "Surely there's not an elephant coming?" Seeming to panic, the Coyote ran to a hole, shouting: "Hurry up! Hurry up! The ground is moving." I thought: "It's not much good going into a hole in the ground if the ground is moving." But the hole wasn't in the ground, it was in the sky and it wasn't so much a hole as a square box. It was like an old safe, the sort that has really thick metal walls, hanging in the sky. The door was missing: bank robbery came to mind. We scrambled up and crouched in this safe in the sky, peering over the edge, watching the ground ripple and buckle.

The Coyote said: "There's going to be a change." And I saw that the trees were the cause of the rippling of the ground. They were going to become Walking Beings and the earth was being shaken like a blanket by the trees pulling up their roots. For as far as I could see, right to the horizon, the green and brown landscape was rolling and heaving because the trees were lifting their legs out of the ground and walking off. The world was full of trees stumping away, stumping off to do their own thing.

He said: "There's going to be a change. Now people are going to be trees. I'll be the ground." And he laid himself down as the yellow ground. I became a tree; my roots went into him and my branches went up. He said: "You can drop seeds on me and I'll grow them for you." I dropped some. They were like sycamore seeds, twirling down, striking the ground and driving themselves into the coyote-soil. I stretched my branches up to the blue sky. I reached towards it with joy. I worshipped the sky. I felt great and still, calm and peaceful. I thought: "Now the squirrels can come and live in me and we shan't want to kill them."

Journeying to the Lower World
Meet your animal. Go through an entrance down into the lower world, look around, find a treasure.

6. Green Eyes

I saw the stepping-stones to the island, but I didn't want to walk across them. The path they made was a lot shorter than before, but still I didn't want to. I was standing to the right of them on the edge of the mainland. The island was quite close and the water looked pretty shallow. Logically, if there were stepping-stones, it would be, so I thought: "I'll wade." I decided to wade because I don't like cold water and I thought it would be good to get into it, good to confront that dislike of getting wet.

The Coyote was already on the island shouting: "Hurry up, hurry up!" He was pacing along the shoreline. Jumping up and down at the water's edge, he seemed frantically over excited. It amused me to see him in such a rush. I felt quite calm and was, for a change, not in a hurry, not setting off ahead of time.

But when the drumming started, I didn't. I hesitated on the shore, asking myself a series of questions: "Shall I take my shoes off?" "Will my clothes get wet?" "Shall I wear my clothes or not?" I was stuck. It was ridiculous: "I'll never get going. I'm going to miss the whole thing. Stop panicking, the shoes don't matter." When I looked down they were made of wood anyway, so I stepped in.

The very next step plunged me into deep water and I began to sink down, down, down. The Coyote dived off the island and came down with me. I was glad about that. Way, way down was the entrance to an underwater cave and we swam in. As we entered the water-filled tunnel I became besotted with the Coyote and I rolled against him, feeling the hairs on his wet coat floating and tickling me, and his strong body cutting through the water carrying us along. I did not want this delight to end. I just wanted to roll along in the water with the Coyote and feel the feelings of it. Eventually, like a life-saver, he took hold of me and, pulling me by my collar, hauled me along. We surfaced in a huge underground cavern and he dragged me up onto the sandy beach. We lay there breathless for a moment, and then we started to play. We rolled around and jumped backwards and forwards over each other, and I was pleading: "More, more, more! I want more. Let it go on. Let it go on." I knew in the back of my mind that I had been instructed to find a treasure and place it in my body to ease a pain, but I didn't want to do that just now.

Suddenly the Coyote stood up and said: "Take out my eyes." His eyes were bright green. I said with horror: "Take out your eyes? I can't. Can't." He shrugged as if I was an idiot and turned himself into the wall of the cave. I looked at the wall and there were two green gemstones sticking out of the sandstone. "Oh!" I thought: "It's still the Coyote trying to trick me," and I picked the gemstones out of the wall. Huh, I couldn't take the eyes while they were in his face, but when he became stone I could. A bit of an academic point, I think. I plucked one out with each hand and I closed my fists over them tight. I wouldn't let them go: they were the Coyote's eyes.

Well, now I was holding the treasures tightly in the palms of my hands, but they weren't yet inside my body as per the instructions. I stood there wondering what to do and I thought: "Maybe I'll just hang onto them and get Alexander to put them into my body when I get back." He had said he would do this if we didn't succeed. How lazy of me: "Am I getting lazy now?"

The sand started to run away under my feet like an hour-glass. I wondered: "Where is the Coyote?" I heard him say: "I am under your feet." I looked down, between my toes the sand was mixing with the water and my feet were sinking. The sand and water became a whirlpool and we were sucked down, down, down. The feeling was as good as swimming through the water along the first tunnel; it was delicious: "May it never end! May it go on, and on, and on!"

But the end came, and we came out of the end like coming out of a shute. There was a pile of coyote-sand and my self all mixed up together. We stood up together in a new land. I recognized that it was the second basement and I thought: "Now, I must put the eyes in." So I took the green eye-stones and put them into my body where my ovaries are, one on either side.

The Coyote stood in front of me, face to face, tall as a man, he said emphatically: "Now, really come with me." And he jumped onto the front of me. It was a shock, and I noticed my consciousness changing radically. I thought: "I'm going to lose this. I'm going to lose it." We travelled together to the darkest, darkest space. When we reached our destination, the green gemstones began to move up my body. I saw them rising up, one on either side, glowing in the darkness, and I saw them enter my eye sockets. I thought: "I'm going to see in a whole new way. I wonder what I am going to see with my new eyes." I peered into the darkness and I tried to see.

I tried to see, and eventually I distinguished a round white shape with two thin lines running away horizontally on either side. I questioned: "What is it? What is it?" I blinked to clear the view, but all I could see was the same white shape. I wondered: "Where is the Coyote in this darkness? Where is he? Where is he?" He replied: "I'm still right in front of you and will you stop staring at one of my vertebrae." Is that what it was? The great mystery!

While I was laughing, he suddenly said: "You try and get us back." Shocked, I said: "I can't. I can't do it. I can't even do one step. I can't even remember what came before the darkness. Let's go back together." So we travelled back. Right back to the beginning, and when we arrived there I pleaded with him: "Let's go again. Let's do that again." And we did the whole thing again. This time it was deeply more enjoyable because the anxiety about doing the task, the problems about the timing, had all gone. Everything had gone except the pleasure of it. The whole journey, we did it again, great! All the tunnelling, all the swimming, all the playing on the beach, all the spiralling down the whirlpool; everything was just fabulous and the joke was still funny as well.

Then the drumming changed and we travelled back. When we got back to the shore, he said to me: "Now you know I love you." I knew what I felt about him, but he had been a bit tricky. I said quietly: "Yes, I do."

<u>Taking a Trip to the Middle World</u>
Go to an island. Meet your animal.
Go through a mist, see what happens.

7. Live Lightly

In deference to the Coyote, and only for that reason, I will tell the story of this middle earth journey in which we human travellers were to search for the lost bits of ourselves.

The drumming started. I stood on a shingle beach, my back to the water, looking at a grey world of mist; I was already on the island. Unable to see ahead, I bent down and picked up a pebble. Then I stepped forwards. It turned out that the mist bank was as thin as picture glass. I stepped through, crouched down, and put the pebble down. I was in a green landscape. I thought: "I'll wait." The Coyote soon arrived. He said: "What are you here for?" His tone was rather abrupt. I replied: "Um, I'm here to find my lost bits." He asked: "Well, what size are they? Are they big, or are they small?" I hesitated: "I don't really know." Sounding resigned, but ready for action, he said: "Right!"

We became very small, so small that the blades of grass were like trees, we looked there. Then we became very large, so large that the blades of grass were like grains of sand and we looked there. Then he took steps. One step we were tiny and the next step we were huge. We walked along like this for a bit, but we didn't find anything. He turned round to me and he said, slowly and deliberately, in a patronizing way: "I showed you that the whole universe is your body, so how can you have lost anything?" It was true: he had showed me this on a previous journey. I felt rather ignorant and slightly embarrassed: "I don't know really." I stood there feeling stupid. There was an awkward pause.

Then I thought of the bungalow that he had renovated for me. I thought of the pub in the first basement. Picking up this thought, he said: "You think that is the middle world, so let's go there." Well, I'd only looked in the door before; I didn't want to spend any time in there, but we went. It was dingy, dark and horrible. There was nobody there. I said: "What are we going to do in here? You know, what have we got to do? What's my task?" He looked at me and said: "Stay here and learn to live lightly." He, meanwhile, perched on a barstool and propped himself up against the end of the bar, a whisky beside him.

I thought: "I suppose, if we have got to stay here, I could make it nicer." So I began to polish the bar. Under the grime, the bar turned out to be made of copper, so that looked nice and shiny. I glanced at the Coyote to see if we could go yet. No go. I pulled up the carpets, took them outside and burnt them. As they smouldered I thought what a good idea it would be to burn this pub down, but then I realized that the fire would probably burn the rest of the bungalow down as well, so I couldn't do that.

Under the ghastly carpeting, there was a fine wooden dance floor. I cleaned the floor and polished it. Then I hung a glitter ball above it. Initially I had thought of having a disco there, but I went off the idea; it would be too noisy upstairs, nevertheless, I hung the glitter ball up. It sparkled. I felt very pleased. The Coyote calmly took out a six-shooter and shot it to smithereens. That was very depressing. I wondered what he meant by 'living lightly', because obviously what I had done wasn't it.

What did he mean by 'living lightly'? Stay in this dreary place amidst all this dreadfulness and be light? Without doing anything? I couldn't quite get it. I thought of turning the dark and dingy pub into a ghost train. People could come in and have a laugh and maybe that was what he meant. But that idea didn't get off the ground.

I thought: "Well, I am the universe. Think, think! Oh, I'm failing here, I'm failing. I AM the Universe. Well, I will expand out of this place." I did do that, I expanded into a huge sphere, but I didn't feel any better, I didn't connect to anything, I didn't know what the point was, so I came back into the pub. I looked hopefully at the Coyote, but he ignored me. I felt very down.

The drum called us back. I had become so depressed by then that I didn't come out of the journey properly. The mist was so thin and the journey was of so little distance that I did know the way back and I didn't come back with the Coyote. He was probably drunk by this time. I came through the mist, forgetting the pebble. Dutifully I went back in, brought it out, and put it back down exactly where I had picked it up.

I lay there on the seminar room floor not understanding the journey at all. I told Alexander so. He said it didn't matter. It mattered to me! I was lying there waiting and I heard the Coyote whisper to me: "You see; you can't even work this life out. You can't even work the middle world out. You don't even know the rules of the middle world. You don't even understand the middle world." And that was the end of that journey.

<u>Travelling to the Upper World</u>
Travel up a mountain with your animal.
Rise up through clouds. Go for it!

8. The Fall

I decided to paddle my own canoe. I paddled out to the left of the island because I want to understand more about the left. I looked up and the afternoon sun was above and ahead. I wanted to paddle on towards the sun, but I had instructions to follow. I stood up in the canoe and made a prayer to the Sun and to the spirit of the Ancient Grandfather. I prayed that I might find something valuable on my journey. I prayed for some insight, some teaching. I put myself in their hands: let them decide.

Then I turned right and landed on the island. On a level plain, a short way inland, the Coyote was standing waiting, taller than a man. I went up to him and took hold of the long shaggy hair on the front of his shoulders. We took off into the sky. We went straight up like a rocket but slower. The way he was loaded, carrying me, reminded me of the space shuttle. I felt I should remind him of the journey instructions, and I said: "We need clouds." In response, he made an atomic mushroom cloud, very small, far beneath us. I was shocked: atomic bomb bursts are not funny. An old, tired joke from childhood began to surface about not mush room inside, but it subsided again without breaking into laughter, and we went higher. I said with urgency: "Coyote, we need clouds." In a resigned tone, he said: "You need clouds?" And he blew clouds out of his mouth filling the sky in every direction. We dutifully passed through them and on into space. We arrived somewhere, a land, a plain, a place. Yes, we spent some time on a landscape. I say 'on' because it felt very temporary, very fragile and very thinly constructed, nonetheless, we rested there.

After a while, far away, up on the left, I saw a Golden Eye in the sky. This was exciting, and I pointed it out to the Coyote. We took off and travelled towards it at speed, flying in through the centre into a golden landscape. We landed in this golden place where everything was drenched in golden light, where everything was dripping in golden dew-light. It is possible that everything was made of golden light. Everything was very, very still, but on the point of something happening.

We were still in the Eye when the Coyote took me on to some other state that I cannot remember at all. A time must have passed and he brought me back. I felt grateful that he had looked after me in there. When we were back in the golden place, he said: "Do you know where you are?" I said carefully: "I am in a state of being." He said: "There is only one Being." There was a long pause.

Then I heard the words: "I am, I am, I am," repeated again and again, like a heartbeat. I had a vague impression that some more bad jokes were attempting to materialize in the space inside the Eye, trying to break up the rhythmic pulse of I am. I remember 'I-am-bic pentameters' and 'Oh, what an ass I am' trying to become funny and burst the quiet atmosphere with their crazy vibrations, but they couldn't break in and they faded away.

The Coyote asked me: "Do you know the first step back?" I knew it would be out through the centre of the Eye, but I didn't speak; silently I went to the hole where the light streams out. The hole was large enough for me to stand upright in the opening, and encircling it there was a concave rim, a bit like a tyre rim turned inside out. This rim was made of gold metal, the gold metal, which I am beginning to think is solid light, condensed light. This rim was slightly wider than I am, and the bevelled edges made a comfortable seat. I sat there, looking out to my right and looking in to my left. Outside was vast, empty, inky black. Inside was hard to describe, sticky, pressing, poised on the point of movement and golden. I understood the outside better than the in.

He asked: "Where are you now?" and I said: "Stuck in the Eye." The double meaning was not lost on me. The Coyote was not stuck; he was to my right, out in space, standing outside the Eye. Suddenly, without a sound and without any shock wave, the Eye blew up, disintegrating into huge chunks. I watched them, tumbling and rolling, as they slowly disappeared in the vastness of space. I felt that the Coyote had made it happen; I reached out and held on to him tightly.

We began to fall. We fell, and fell, and fell, and fell, and fell. I was surprised to notice that I was enjoying it. It was dark and clear, delightful. Then came the thought: "What if he plays a trick on me now and disappears? Don't even think that thought. Don't even allow that thought." So I pushed it away. We fell for ages upon ages upon ages. We landed softly. I landed on my back and he landed on top of me; there was hardly a bump. The instant we hit the ground the drum beat changed and he said kindly: "There, was that alright?"

The drumming had changed to the beat for coming back, but we didn't move. We were back. Or was I? I couldn't go back through the journey: there was no way I could reverse that fall. The Coyote didn't bring me out, and I didn't get back to the island. I was where we landed, flat on my back on the ground.

As I was lying in a fairly quiet state of consciousness on the floor of the seminar room, while other people were making notes, these words came into my head: "Are you going to stay where you was, or are you going to come back to where you are not?"

>(On this day secret atomic tests were carried out in India.
>Nice coincidence, Coyote.)

THREE

Flexible Boundaries

The Four Beings

Walking the Tight Rope

Coyote Goes to Hollywood

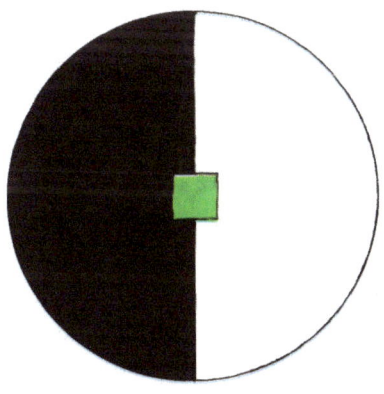

> Contacting the Power Animal
> Go to a favourite place in nature.
> An animal will meet you there. Go with it!

9. Flexible Boundaries

It was the first journey of the seminar week. As we prepared I glanced at the medicine altar, always at the centre of our human circle when we worked together. The wings of a small bird lay there. One day, when I was meditating at home, I had heard the tell-tale thump of a bird hitting the window of my room. Later I found it, dead, on the pavement below the window. It was a Treecreeper, a bird that uses its curved beak to clean the trees of the insects that live in their bark. I had kept the wings and tail as a gift and, attaching them to a piece of bark, I had made a medicine totem with them in the shape of a T-cross; the small wings horizontal, the long flexible tail vertical. I looked intently at them now, and I felt the subtle colours of their tree-bark designs enter my consciousness in a special way.

The drumming started. Immediately I heard the impact of the bird on the glass. It lay dead on the pavement below my window. I was in it, and it was in me. Dead on the pavement on the main street through the village, this was hardly a favourite place in nature.

The bird and I resurrected ourselves by travelling back through time. We rose up to the window pane and, travelling in reverse, went backwards, way back, through the yew tree across the road, and way, way back, back to the ash tree in the gulley on the local moorland, the Fell. We landed high on a branch that grows out over the water. I clung to the bark, like a Treecreeper does, and began to search for insects lurking below.

The first insect I ate was the Coyote. I saw a flash of yellow as he disappeared. I saw him, a split second later I swallowed him. I thought: "Oh dear, I didn't even greet him!" It would be complicated now he was inside me and, in order to meet him, I had to invert myself by going in through my own mouth and down into my own body. I entered. My blood vessels, capillaries and corpuscles were like branches, twigs and leaves. I met the Coyote in the canopy of the tree. Beyond the branches of the tree there was darkness; he was going in that direction, upwards.

We broke out into the blackness and we played. We ran about and jumped up and down and never ran into any boundaries. I investigated, and I found that the edges of the blackness were flexible and invisible. There were boundaries, but, no matter how acrobatic I became, I never ran into them.

While we were there, the Coyote told me that he had hidden something for me to find. Eagerly I said: "Shall I look for it now?" But he said: "You won't find anything I hid for you in five minutes! You've got the whole seminar to look." Nevertheless, I did have a quick look. I am nearly seeing it now. It's got a greenish glow and it shows up in the darkness.

I wanted to talk more with the Coyote; there was time and space and little pressure. I said: "Coyote, I'm sorry I never greeted you properly. How can I demonstrate that I love you? Because I don't think feeling it is enough, that seems a selfish thing, how can I show you?" And he replied: "You follow me." We moved towards a distant circle of golden light surrounded by the dark. As we prepared to enter, the drumming changed and we had to come back. While everybody else was writing notes, I went to the edge of that circle and looked in.

Journeying to the Lower World
Meet your animal. Go through an entrance down
into the lower world, look around, find a treasure.

10. The Four Beings

I stood at the front door of the bungalow waiting for the drumming to start. When it began, I walked to the gulley in the north and I stopped at the entrance to the cave that is there. I felt the presence of the Coyote. I looked down and I was standing on a patch of yellow ground: this would be the Coyote. The ground began to slip towards the cave entrance. Sliding in and descending, I let him take me down.

We arrived underground in a cavern so huge there seemed to be no floor, ceiling, or sides; suspended in the centre there was a square blanket-like piece of ground floating in space. On it there were four ...., well, maybe they were Beings, but they weren't like any Beings I was familiar with. One sat on each of the four corners of the blanket. They were all the same colour, light reddish-brown; all the same texture, like carved wood; all the same shape, rising up from their bases and curving inwards towards the centre, then bending over and ending in a downward curl. I thought: "They ARE Beings and I could speak to them." But it all began to change.

They went black and grew upwards into a huge column that was like the most incredibly complicated mace head you could ever see, or like a blackened petrified tree, spiky, chunky and immobile, not like a living tree. This black object became absolutely huge. Then it slowly tipped over and, lying horizontally, hung there in space, looking like the spaceship from the film 2001, except that its origin was organic. I was completely knocked out by it. It was unimaginable, and I hadn't got a clue what it was, so I looked around to ask the Coyote.

The object was immense and I felt my normal size, but when I found the Coyote, he was minute. I thought: "He is so small I can't communicate with him, and I'm going to lose him in a minute unless I do something. If I become smaller than he is, then he will seem big." So, concentrating on the grain of Coyote, I shrank myself down alongside the huge unknown object until he was bigger than me. He seemed comfortingly large now, his spine pressed along the side of the cavern, his body a sinuous curve. I was deeply relieved to see him like this. Hanging over me, he said: "We will go forward."

In the distance, cutting through the middle of the field of view, a thin golden horizontal line was visible. Together we travelled towards it through the darkness. As we got closer a white dot became apparent, marking the central point. We aimed right for that spot. We went through the hole that was there and into a flickering world of black, white, black, white, black, white.

As the colours shifted from black to white, white to black, black to white, the drum beat became more and more intense. The experience was visually and audibly unnerving. It confused my eyes, my ears and my thoughts. I couldn't think. I couldn't think where we could be. The Coyote helped me: "This is choice." He said: "This is it. This is it. Find choice here." .... "Oh, this is what he has hidden for me to find." .... "O-oh, here we are in this black and white flickering space, and I have to find choice."

I looked and looked and I saw a speck of green. I remembered the green flash in the burnt out forest; this time it felt more tangible. I concentrated hard, cutting the black and white alternating lights out of my mind, looking only at the minute moment between the two. In those minute moments I found a little square of green; it was about six inches across. The Coyote said: "That's choice." I looked at him and I said: "Oh, shall I fold it or roll it?" We both burst out laughing because that was a choice; I had made it more complicated already. I thought: "I must put this in my body to carry it safely, so how shall I do that?" He quipped: "Eat it, you usually do!" This was said with irony because I had recently eaten him, but I followed his advice.

That was good fun, but now, now that there was nothing to do, the black and the white alternating to the drum beat became very, very oppressive, like a strobe light penetrating right into my being. I couldn't shut them out any more, and I dreaded the next beat of the drum; flickering colours and drum beat in perfect synchrony. I had never disliked the sound of the drum before and this made me feel sad. I began to feel very ill. I said to the Coyote: "I don't think I can stand this place any longer." He said: "Move to the left with me."

We moved together, out of the abrupt switching from black to white, into a place where black and gold moved together in smooth, undulating waves, like shallow black water, pushed forward by a gentle tide, rippling onto a sandy shore. The drum beat sounded completely different now, soft and melodious. I could hear two notes, one of which was continuous and hummed beneath the regular beat.

We walked a long way out in the shallow sea so that we were surrounded by the velvety calm. We got into a conversation where I said how much I enjoyed travelling with him. In reply, he said: "You can travel with me forever." I said something like: "I will. Well, at least until the end of this journey!" That was my attempt at detachment, but, actually, I didn't want to leave that place ever. Being there with him I felt something more than happiness so strongly, something amazing and completely as it should be. We walked slowly on the path, which was made of the black and gold bands, and we seemed to be walking into infinity. I decided I would like to die there, and I began to try to die. But he knew I didn't want to go back and he diminished himself. I didn't want to stay there then, and I capitulated: "Ok, we will walk back."

We went back through all the stages until we came out through the white hole. I got lost there. The Coyote was with me; even so I could not remember the next bit. I said: "You have brought us out this far, and I can't remember what happened before this, so please, Coyote, show me." Nothing happened. I had a moment's panic. Then I realized that, although I might not know where I was in the journey, I did know exactly where I was in my body. I was just coming up above the diaphragm. I noticed that my right arm was paralysed and I said to the Coyote in a matter-of-fact way: "My right arm is paralysed, and it has gone black." He replied: "You have choice now. What do you want to do?"

I expanded my awareness into my whole body, it was all black, and as my awareness expanded my body began to rise. The sensation of rising was so extraordinary that for a moment I thought I was levitating. I thought: "That'll give the drummer a shock, if I rise three inches off the ground." But really I knew that it was another body rising, and that was my choice, that rising was a going back to somewhere, to something, I'd known before, and there I saw a flash of red. The minute that I saw the red flash I knew where we were in the journey, and I realized that it was the Four Extraordinary Beings that I had completely lost the memory of; we were in the place where I had first seen them.

The Coyote quickly took me outside the cavern and, as quickly, brought me back in. He only took me out to show me the beginning of the journey then he took me back in to where these Beings were sat on the ...., well, I can only describe it as a blanket, but it was the Earth really. I looked at them for some time. I wondered if I could communicate with them, or if I couldn't. I asked the Coyote, and he said: "Ask them a question." I looked at them, and I said slowly: "Who are you?" At that very second the drum beat changed to sound the return. This was ironic and funny; the timing was so surprising: "Who are you?" and, bang, I had to come back.

When I was out on the gold and black seashore I had no desire to leave, like I said, I thought about dying out there. That was pointless because dying wouldn't maintain the experience either, and I did wonder how I could retain that blissful state. In the period of silence after the last drum beat, the Coyote came and talked to me. He said: "You know I could be with you all the time, here, on this level." I couldn't believe it, and I had a chronic headache. He said: "If you had faith in me, I could take that headache away." I struggled to believe it, and I tried harder to move into that belief space. As I succeeded, the headache disappeared. Then, as my rationality and my scepticism fought back, I felt myself losing it and the headache returned. We went for it again; the headache went again, and again came back. So, I didn't manage to bring the Coyote here to be with him full time, but I know the headache came and went, and that is something that I can achieve.

Taking a Trip to the Middle World
Go to an island. Meet your animal.
Go through a mist, see what happens.

11. Walking the Tight Rope

Waiting for the journey to begin this evening, I felt completely spaced out and deeply involved in the colour brown. There was a painful gash in my chest, and I looked through the hole into other worlds. I also worried: "I ought to be preparing to go to an island, but the only island I can think of is the one I saw in the clouds at sunset earlier this week."

All my thoughts seem, and I feel, totally divorced from the Coyote. He is not very happy with me. I made a mistake at lunchtime running around with a friend to sort out where to stay after the seminar ends. While we were busy doing that, I saw the Coyote tight-roping across Niagara Falls. He said: "Walk the tight rope of your integrity across the Niagara Falls of your ego." The image of him crossing the falls made me laugh and I shared it with my friend; at once my integrity told me that I had made a mistake. Then the Coyote got angry with me and told me off. He asked me if I thought I was clever. Back in the group after lunch, someone said something very clever, and he whispered: "You see, you're not even as smart as that. Don't think you're clever, not even as smart as that. I think you should keep your mouth shut." The ticking-off went on and on; all the rest of the afternoon he would unexpectedly nip me and scold me again. I took the punishment because I knew I had spoken when I didn't need to. I shouldn't have run around at lunchtime, I'd rather have lain still. I'll lie still now!

The drumming began, and I realized that the brown I could see was the brown of the feathers on the back of a Golden Eagle. So, contrary to all instructions, I decided I would fly with the Eagle to the cloud island in the sky; I climbed on. The Eagle took off and flew like a boat that was sailing through the water of the air to a land in the sky.

When I stepped ashore the Coyote was there, hardly visible, hardly an essence, difficult to catch. He wasn't making it easy for me. The light was dark and I called out: "I have followed you through the darkness before and it was terribly difficult."

I followed him into a landscape that was purple and green, very bright, all in rounded mounds hugging close to the ground. All this time my body was heaving and changing shape. The realm that was swelling up in this green and purple land was the lower left-hand side. Best not to give those strange feelings too much attention, so I shifted my vision over to the right and I stared at the minute details close to the ground. Tiny green vibrant shoots were rising, and I realized that the Coyote had led me to the internal landscape of lavender, an enormous space of green and purple vibrations and shoots that sing.

Then we moved together over to the left again, higher up. As we crossed over, I wondered: "Is this play as we were instructed?" Before the journey, we had been given an extra instruction to experiment with playfulness, so I said to the Coyote quite sharply: "Is this play?" and he replied: "This is interesting, and that's the only way you know how to play."

My body was changing shape constantly, swelling up and shrinking down. It was not my physical body, obviously, it was another body, and I didn't understand what was going on. I felt that the journey had moved quite out of my experience, and I was really struggling to identify anything, even to see anything. Seeing and identifying are clearly connected to each other: if I couldn't interpret it then I couldn't 'see' it because I couldn't give it a recognisable form in my conscious mind. So, I imagined, the act of seeing a thing must also limit it. I didn't know. I knew a few things though. I knew we had just moved out of the lavender and into another world.

We entered a world that was chalky. It was white, granular and vertical, whereas the previous world had been horizontal. We were moving around in this new world when I went through a gap in between two sinuous roots that intertwined. I paused there a millisecond too long; they grew, they expanded, and they trapped me by the waist. I looked at the Coyote for help, and he said: "You can get out of that. I've shown you how to change your body shape." So I got on with it.

Other people taking journeys in the seminar room were making a lot of noise. I was aware of it. Someone was even snoring loudly and that was very funny. It was funny even though it was very, very hard to hang onto the thread of my trip. After I escaped from the roots, I got slightly diverted by the snoring, but it didn't bring me out.

We moved across to the right into a black world. I started to try and make sense of it because, as we went into each place, I had to sort out the images from the colour and try and form an opinion of where I was. Some game, more like an exercise in brain-melt!

In this black world there was a singular thing, not dissimilar to the black mace-like object in the previous journey but smaller, squat and compact. It occupied a circular space and sat in a dish-shaped depression. I couldn't possibly imagine what it was; it was incomprehensible. It looked like the beginning of some peculiar plant, but again, almost like coal, black shiny pressure-formed coal. Looking beyond this strange thing, I saw light ahead; the black world, in which the unknown object was placed, was a cave. To reach the entrance I had to pass close by the object. As I inched past, in trepidation hugging the outer wall, I felt a force field emanating from object acting upon me like strong magnetic attraction. I reached the entrance intact and looked out.

I saw a gold and blue world beyond, beautiful, a world into which I wanted to move when abruptly the drum beat changed to call us back. I felt that I could take a step, out of the cave, into the blue and gold world, and journey back another way. It seemed like a short cut; I could see the starting place of the journey almost as if we had gone in a circle and were nearly back at the beginning. I was very tempted to go out there and nip across to the beginning, but something said: "No, do not go that way."

Partly it was recalling Alexander's instructions and partly it was the whispering Coyote, and so I did not leave the cave. We came back the correct way, working our way back through the realms. But I was only in the green and purple world when the drumming stopped, and I continued to move back slowly while other people were writing. I had to move slowly because coming back was equally as hard work as travelling out had been.

The session was ending; everybody was drifting away. I opened my eyes so that anybody who was interested might think I was there, but I wasn't. When most people had left the room I went away on the trip again, and I went down with the Coyote into a yellow-ochre world. It was long in a vertical sense, smooth, columnar, a slippery, muddy kind of place. As we slithered down this world, I experimented with different states of consciousness. I played with the differences between trance travelling and dreaming, the difference, for instance, between trance sight and dream images, and the difference in body sensations between conscious dreaming and dreaming when asleep.

The body sensations particularly interested me. I found that in trance I could feel very ill, especially when undergoing changes of state, but my physical body was not in pain, only another body might suffer. On the other hand, if I tried to hold on to my conscious mind while going to sleep my physical body would begin to feel very bad indeed, my brain would get dizzy and start to fall out of itself, and my physical body would feel sick. This made me wonder about how many bodies there are. Eventually, I went to step in among some trees and I realized that I had stepped into a dream so I woke myself up and came back.

When I got back into my body, I found that the split at the right side of my breastbone was still open, and it was hurting. It was hurting a lot. I could see it there, all jagged at the edges. I tried to close it, but I couldn't. That pain started this morning, and now it turns out to be caused by the fallout with the Coyote. I wanted to make up with him, but I couldn't crawl. I couldn't just say sorry; it seemed that I had to have a snapping fight with him. I hate fighting and I said: "Well, can't I just love you? I can't fight and love." He replied: "Treat fight as a kind of play; you won't be any different." He said something like that; it was confusing. If I snapped with aggression was that the back of me? That is a very strange sentence, and I feel I have missed some vital understanding of this process. Anyway, we must have fought, I must have snapped back, but maybe because I would not willingly do that in my daily life I have refused to remember it.

While I was on the journey I felt as if nothing would ever make sense again. That feeling has passed off now. At first lower body things blew up, moved around like balloons and deflated again, but as the journey went on, the body shape changes diminished. Basically, I don't know what was going on. It's as if I am entering a whole new zone of travelling. For some purpose, I hope. Yes, I had to trust the Coyote, even though we had fallen out, and just try and follow him. As I lay here it came to me that the Coyote holes up here, and through him I can look out into wholeness. He told me: "You never find the edge of wholeness."

<u>Travelling to the Upper World</u>
Travel up a mountain with your animal.
Rise up through clouds. Go for it!

12. Coyote Goes to Hollywood

Alexander had decided to travel on this journey too, so we would not be journeying with the drum but to a CD of orchestral music. I lay down early to get ready, snug under a blanket, and became very calm, waiting for the brand new experience of travelling to music.

When the music started, I found myself standing looking

at the front of the bungalow. It was overgrown with greenery and seemed half sunk into the ground. The doorway was now a trilithon. I looked with interest: the bungalow was getting quite prehistoric. I noticed that two Coyotes had arrived, a golden-yellow one on my left and a black one on my right. I had met them before, but they had not appeared together in any previous seminar journeys. The force emanating from them was wonderful, and we greeted each other with joy. We raised our arms, our hands touched, we formed a three-sided pyramid; we twisted together, danced together and loved each other deeply. I was so glad to see them I nearly cried. It was excellent.

Then I remembered that we needed to go to the mountain. I knew that there was a mountain to the east of the bungalow. I thought we could fly there, so we rose up onto the flat roof of the bungalow and I attempted to go towards the east, but I found myself turned around by the Coyotes and they pointed me in the opposite direction. I was facing the west, and the sun was setting. In unison, we moved in that direction. As we travelled, I saw an amazing picture of a bright sky, with a dark sun sinking down below the horizon, while I was admiring it we came to a dead halt. To my surprise, we had hardly moved at all, and we lay down on our backs on the roof of the bungalow to take a rest, the black one to my right, the yellow one to my left. I was glad to have the chance to express my love and gratitude to them; I turned first to the Black Coyote and poured love towards him.

At that time Alexander came from the tape machine to lie down. I lay there listening. I experimented; I sent out feelers to touch him, just scanning really. Then a strange and very powerful shuddering feeling came into the top of my right shoulder and travelled all the way down that side of my body. It felt like a force had crossed over from him, and in response I gave him the Black Coyote. Once, on a journey deep into the ground, I met an old woman in a market place and I would not give him to her. I told her I had no money to buy her goods and I wouldn't give the Black Coyote away for trinkets, but I gave him to my Teacher. I could do this because after travelling with the Black Coyote for some months, I understood that I had, in a sense, made him. He was the product of my knowledge and power from my entire existence. He was part of me, but the Yellow Coyote was a different creature, a power animal outside of me, so that gift was given.

Then I thought that, wonderful as it was right there, I couldn't stay there because I was supposed to be travelling. I tried to look at the mountain and to go there. I tried to go, and I tried to go. I couldn't get away. The Coyote was standing off to the left watching me. I was assuming he would come with me, but I just could not move. I struggled: "Have I got to admit defeat? Am I to lie here beside Alexander, go nowhere, and accept it?" I didn't know. I just thought: "Oh......!" Then I gave up and lay back down there.

The Coyote came and stood over me. Cocking his head to one side, he said quizzically: "Why are you trying to go to the mountain, can't you see that you are already on top of it?" I looked down and, sure enough, I was on the top of a mountain. I could see both east and west, and two suns were rising; a sun was rising in the east, and a sun was rising in the west. The suns rose into the blue sky. Forming a magnificent arch, they met and merged at the zenith. It was a beautiful image, and I watched to see what it might become. It was briefly a golden feathered head-dress, then it became an open circle, and the Coyote's face appeared within it. It reminded me of something that I used to watch in the cinema; it was like the beginning of the Pathé News when the cockerel crows outrageously loud. The Coyote was looking down out of the circle, pulling a ridiculous face, and a rainbow went down from either side of the circle to touch the ground far below.

Standing on the mountain looking up to the Coyote, I was very small. He was laughing so much that I stretched out my arms and jumped up to be with him. He caught me in his mouth and swallowed me, and that was so great because once I had accidentally eaten him and now he was eating me.

I went sliding down his throat, and I wondered: "What's going to happen now?" I arrived in his guts. They were blue and gold; I had entered the blue and gold world that I had so wanted to step into on the previous journey. It began as a great sky-scape of blue sky, and clouds coloured gold by the sun. Then it became more geometric, a horizontal world of alternating blue and gold bars looking something like the head-dress of a Pharaoh, and I got understanding of this blue and gold world; I was inside the Coyote, I was in coyote-land, a Hollywood phantasy land, right inside it.

I was standing there, slightly to the left of the picture, when I noticed a huge Black Housefly; compared to me it was like an elephant. It was standing to my right, and, by way of introduction, it said: "I am the hoover of this world. I clean this world." I thought: "That's totally the reverse of our world, because in our world flies are considered to be dirty things." But he replied: "No, no, through my proboscis I suck up all the dirty, germy things in the spirit world." Then, to his right, I noticed a White Maggot; compared to me she was the size of a whale. She introduced herself to me: "And I eat all the flesh in this world. I get rid of all the flesh so that none of it can contaminate the spirit world." I found them both very agreeable; they were wonderful creatures, industrious, charming and gentle; gentle, gentle, the black and the white.

I looked around again at the blue and gold world, and, in the distance far ahead, I noticed the most enormous statue. It looked like a Hollywood film-set representation of the Great Spirit; over large, a bit too glitzy, golden coloured head to toe. The film Cleopatra had nothing on this; this was a bit too, too glamorous, a bit too Busby Berkeley, but it was awesome at the same time. I enjoyed it. It filled me with joy! It filled me with joy, but at the same time I could see that, towering above me, maybe fifty feet tall, it was kind of garish. High above I could see the cheerful, beneficent face looking down, smiling broadly, surrounded by a feathered head-dress made all of gold. The feathers were a little too rounded and a little too smooth to be like real feathers, but the overall effect was of great friendliness.

Rising slowly in the air, I ran my hands over the golden smoothness, over the rotund belly. Whoops, the statue had a large belly button! It was a round hole, an entrance, and the Void was through there. It was enticing, but I did not rush to go through because it was so comfortable where I was, so smoothly golden was the outside of this Great Being. Eventually I did enter into the blackness of the Void and, clear as a bell as it was then, I seem to have forgotten the lot. I do remember thinking as I went through: "I am leaving the Coyote outside. I hope he'll come and get me if I call him." As a safety measure, I shouted: "Please, Coyote, come and get me when it is time."

Once in the Void, I played some games and made some experiments, had things appear and disappear, and changed day to night and night to day. Then I experienced some dizzy spinning sensations, and I wondered: "Maybe it is time to get back." As if on cue, the Coyote pushed his nose through the belly button of the Great Spirit. Remembering that he had swallowed me, I marvelled: "That's a clever trick, because he is now inside his own body pushing his nose into the Void." But I was concentrating on getting out, and I wondered how to deal with the situation; his nose was like a plug. I caught hold of a whisker, and I managed to climb under his top lip. I wasn't sure if this was an entirely good idea; it was still quite black up there inside his lips, but I felt that when he pulled his nose out of the hole I too would get out of the Void. At that moment I bumped into his eyetooth, gleaming white in the darkness, I put my arms around it and hung on.

That's what happened, and we were back. I admired the Great Spirit some more. Well, I admired the facade of the Great Spirit, the Coyote creation of the Great Spirit. Eventually I thought: "Time to go now." Although I can't remember seeing the black fly and the white maggot on the way out, I slowly went back through all that had happened; I travelled through the blue and golden world, out through the Coyote's mouth, and back onto the top of the mountain. The suns split and went down.

As I eased myself into my body, I could feel myself sinking into an inert carcass. Then I felt the same physical sensation all down my right side that I felt at the beginning, Alexander's aura, or whatever it was. I don't know what it was. It was like a shudder that went down. It was really great: shudders can be great. I had just settled in quite nicely when the music finished, perfect timing.

FOUR

The Seven Jewels

The Whole Secret

Visiting the Celestial City

> The Healing Quest
> Ask the power animal
> for advice, help or a gift.

13. The Seven Jewels

I felt very meditative and deeply relaxed. The contact with the Coyote started, and, in order not to think about the journey until after it was over, I hid under the wings of an owl. They made a perfectly enclosed, quiet, still space, like a low tent, for me to sit in. I sat there and waited. There was no necessity to do anything. The drumming started. I met the Coyote as I had planned at a great pile of red leaves.

I suddenly felt anxious, and he said: "Shut your eyes and let me lead you." He led me gently to the right, down what seemed like a tunnel, but it was a gap between the wall of a cave and an object. I suspected it was the shiny black object from the black world in the previous middle world journey; my eyes were shut but I felt this, the force field was similar. This time it was a tight squeeze, but it didn't take very long and immediately we were through I opened my eyes.

Yellow light was everywhere. I looked into the yellow light and everything was crystal clear and exactly as it should be. We were in a great golden space that I knew was the solar plexus. In the middle of this energy centre a golden object was forming. It looked like the barrel of an anti-aircraft gun from the second world war; it was long and thin and had various bumps down its length, but it was not a gun barrel; there was no hole through the centre, it was solid. I looked at it for some time, but could get no further with what it might be.

It came to me that this visit to the bright, clear light of the solar plexus was the Coyote's gift. Remembering the instructions for the journey, I asked him for some advice about the difficulties I have in relationships. In response, he showed me yellow and then he showed me black; the contrast between the two made their individual qualities more definite. He made it clear that was exactly how it was in our world and it couldn't be any other way. I had seen the colours black and yellow together many times in altered states, but now he showed me how they operated in the everyday world of our conscious life, as night and day, as me and you. I felt

I understood that opposites had to interact in a creative world, but the constant change they brought often upset me. He asked me what I was feeling and I said: "I preferred it when it was all black." I laughed: my attitude was pathetic, pathetic but genuinely expressed.

It was my turn to give a gift; I had nothing with me but an idea, so I sat us down cross-legged, facing each other, very close together, and I began to pass my seven jewels to him. One by one, I took them carefully out of my energy centres and put them carefully into his. As I did that, the energy flowed between us because, when precious things are given in such circumstances, it is always an exchange; it has been proved to me on several occasions that this is the case, but it is still also the case that the decision to give can be hard.

First, I gave him the jewel from the energy centre in my brain, a feeling too mysterious to describe. Second, I transferred the jewel from my centre of seeing, and felt the golden energy of these two centres running smooth and straight between us in both directions simultaneously. Next, I took out the throat jewel, and put it in his throat. Here the energy went out from me to him, and then it came back from him to me. In the heart centre, there was no feeling of energy moving between, just a peaceful pool of shared energy as we rested together there. In the solar plexus the energy exchange came in surges; there were two channels and the energy ran from me to him through one, and from him to me through the other; both pulsing at the same time in opposite directions. I took the jewel from the centre of generation, and this jewel was green. All the way down through the other centres the jewel of energy had been golden, in the generative centre it was green. In this centre, the energy circulated in a figure of eight, one ribbon of energy circulating round two fixed points.

Then I knew that the time for the journey was coming to an end. I reached for the jewel of the root centre and that was black. Time was running out. I looked at the Coyote, and I thought: "Hum, I'll give him a bit of a shock and put this jewel up his bum, a good place for it, right at the base of his spine." I pushed it in with a pop.

We both hooted with laughter in enjoyment of this joke and this successful transfer of jewellery.

Immediately the last jewel was in, the drum beat changed and I came back, easily, easily, travelling with the Coyote, separate but together. I got back and I felt great, a great trip. I might as well give up worrying and being unhappy in the trails of relationships. I have decided: "Stop chasing after a relationship you have only heard rumours of, that you have never experienced and that probably wouldn't suit you." I feel liberated. When we had talked in the seminar group of what healing we were seeking for ourselves this week, I dwelt specifically on the relationships I have had with my partners over the years, how I always hid half my nature, how my partners always seemed to think everything was ok while I felt I was having a hard time. Well, today I have seen the lights.

<u>Journey to the Inner Temple</u>
Find inner healing and healing power.

14. The Whole Secret

Somehow I understood that we were to travel without the power animals. This may have been a misunderstanding on my part. I thought Alexander said that they were confined to the lower centres and wouldn't reach the inner temple. I must have got it wrong for some deep reason, because otherwise I would have questioned the instruction as it went against all my inner experience. But I didn't question it; I struggled to follow what I thought we were told.

I found the idea of travelling without the Coyote difficult. I decided: "I'll go back to the place that marked the beginning of my spiritual connection this year. I'll go to the velvet blackness of the temple sanctuary, to the memories of Khemet, the Black Land of Ancient Egypt." It began.

In the distance, higher up and on the left, I saw a long procession. The standard, which led the procession, was the head of a jackal. It seemed to be a funeral procession. I felt confused. It seemed to be a burial ritual, nothing to do with the sanctuary that I intended to get to.

While I was wondering why I couldn't go where I wanted,

I found myself as a dead leaf, dry and curled, floating on a fast flowing stream. The leaf was carried to a place where the water dropped over a low waterfall. I felt the current strengthen, and I knew that the river would soon run underground. I felt I couldn't make that journey without the Coyotes; I called out and they came to support me as we were swept under the water and through the rock: not into an entrance in the rock as into a temple, but through the rock into the centre of the rock which was a temple.

We were standing in stone. I could sense the surface far above. The Coyotes were puzzled, and didn't seem to be willing to take the journey upwards. I found myself rising alone with too much of my intellect working. I rose up into a clearing surrounded by beautiful trees.

A deer stepped towards me, the same deer that once visited the bungalow, and, with her, she brought the same pearl that she brought me then. I looked at it closely; it was cloudy and grey, not as beautiful as it had been before. I remembered what my Grandmother used to say: "Pearls improve by wearing." I felt that the pearl had not had enough bodily contact with me, so I took it and placed it on my heart. Slowly I became the ground of the clearing; slowly I became the earth. The grass that was growing out of the earth fed the deer. I stayed like that for a long time, sending up little green shoots and the deer was nibbling.

The clearing grew bigger, and other animals started to cross it. A bear came across first, then, because my intellect was still active, I thought of other animals, and they came and crossed the clearing, disappearing into the trees on the other side. I felt their individual footfalls as they walked across me. There were badgers, foxes, rabbits, little birds, and black beetles. But still my intellect was too....., well, it wasn't like journeying with the Coyote, I felt my own consciousness was too present, and I was feeling rather disappointed with myself. I tried and tried to shed my rational mind.

Suddenly I felt a radical shift of consciousness. I felt my whole body change, and I felt a magical dropping into the back, the very, very deep back lobes of my brain, and sinking down through levels upon levels of darkness. I must have sunk out of consciousness because I lost it. Maybe some time passed. Then in the blackness I heard my voice say: "Oh, my God, I know the whole secret of the Universe!" This statement amazed me, and my being became so excited that I said it again emphatically: "Oh, my God, I know the whole secret of the Universe!"

The shock was so great that, as I heard myself repeat this sentence, I came back into another level of consciousness, a level which was miles away from that place where I knew-what-I-knew. It delighted me vastly to think that I had that knowledge somewhere in my Being, however, the chances of bringing it back were nil. I tried to re-enter that state of 'unconsciousness' where I felt that knowing, but I couldn't get back there, so I lay enjoying the knowledge that I knew something that I couldn't know here. I realized that the only things from beyond that I could clearly know here were at the level of meeting the deer, and cherishing the pearl that the deer gave me. That was the level at which I could most easily connect into the knowledge that I had-and-had-not.

So that was it, a strange journey, very difficult at the beginning. It seemed to me as if I moved first through my conscious history in time, although I only saw the start of that journey in Khemet. Then, it seemed to me as if I moved through my complete history in nature, through the water and into the stone, and up through the ground and into the grass, and into all the animate variety of nature. By becoming the earth that the animals walked upon and fed upon, by becoming that clearing in the forest where the sun shone down, I had done that. I felt as if I was deliberately held with my normal consciousness intruding, and then I was plunged to a vaster depth to learn that I know it all somewhere.

Next Steps Journey
Use your imagination!

15. Visiting the Celestial City

This journey was going to be taken to music. As Alexander talked to us, I wasn't attending to the instructions because the black fly and the white maggot had arrived. The black fly was on the right side of my brain and the white maggot was on the left. They were eating my brain away. They ate it away till there was nothing left but the newel post of the bungalow, and the Coyote sitting cross-legged with his back against it. I ran towards him with joy in my heart and we joined together from the top down.

When our feet merged, the music started and brought us swiftly to the heart centre. This centre was blue below, and we rose up through the blue into gold. Then we rose up out of the body and went into a new spirit plain, where we stood side by side, thinking about what to do. Many things were visible close at hand that I could have looked at, but in the far distance there was a Golden City that drew my attention. Surrounded by gated golden walls, it had many turrets and exotic towers with rounded tops.

As we prepared to travel towards it, the Coyote indicated to me that I should no longer look ahead, so we joined together in the most difficult conjunction, which is back to back, spinal columns together, looking in opposite directions. Standing upright, he travelled forwards, carrying me, behind him, looking backwards. It was novel for me to relinquish control in this way and not try to see what was coming next. By using my peripheral vision, I could see things appearing; then I could observe them as we travelled past and, as they receded into the distance, I could continue to watch them for a long time. He told me that this was the way to see things as they really are, and I noticed that it was a lot less stressful.

We entered the Golden City. We travelled over the many streets till we reached an open space where a golden temple stood. We entered through the double doors. Inside was an enormous statue of a Blue Man, which was as tall as the space within. We entered the statue; it was gold, solid gold with an outer coating of blue. In there, we rested.

I knew, from looking out of my eyes at the back of the Coyote, that I had access to the Coyote's mind, a part he was sharing with me. It was like opening the back of a gold watch. I moved through it examining the interlocking cogs and the intricate movements. I thought of the model of the Newtonian universe, a perfectly made machine, but, no, the metaphor here was a brain that could not be eaten by maggots. This was the spirit mind, a golden mechanism of spirit.

After resting a while, we travelled on over fields. He was travelling horizontally now, running on all fours, and I lay on his back, looking upwards. He told me that I could rest while he carried me, so I shut my eyes and, feeling myself approaching sleep, I thought: "Hum, the trick here is not to fall asleep, but to enjoy this secure feeling that some Being I totally love is in charge."

We passed through another barrier into a spherical world where he wasn't to be the head of me, and I wasn't to be behind. But how could that be in the way that we were joined together? It was like this: from the centre of the sphere the distance to any point on the surface was the same, and we became pulsating waves of light that emanated from the centre; a wave of Coyote, a wave of myself, a wave of Coyote, a wave of myself, only distinguished from each other by subtly different shades of gold, that slight variation was all that defined the pulses of light that came from the centre.

The next task in this quest was to travel to the centre of the centre. This was the next move in this almost-not-optional journey. I couldn't think how to do it. We were outward pulses, so how could we manifest the power to move inwards? We couldn't travel on these pulses as if they were waves on a beach because it was a spherical pulsation and the planes of movement to help us return to the centre were not there. I did not know how to do it. I was thinking about it for a long time, finally I asked the Coyote: "How are we going to do this?" He shot two silver cords out of the palms of his hands; they hooked onto the centre point of the centre and turned into a rope ladder. I thought: "I could do that too, but I'll use the Coyote's ladder and climb up behind him. I'll stick with him." We climbed the ladder towards the centre. It wasn't up; it seemed more horizontal. It was wherever direction had gone. We climbed through a small black hole that was the absolute centre, and stood there looking around.

Then the Coyote unhitched the ladder and threw it away. This was too much for me and I really freaked out. My solar plexus knotted and I thought I might scream. I was horrified, horrified. Now, since I have been thinking about it, I have understood that my extreme reaction was because I have always had an escape route; always planned a life full of endless possibilities that I have thought of in advance; if this: then that; I could take this direction, or I could take that direction, or, if it doesn't work out, I'll retreat to this point here, pick up my stores, and, you know, go on. The Coyote threw the ladder away: it was absolutely horrendous.

Anyway, when I got over feeling sorry for myself, got over the panic, or whatever it was that made it so shocking, I thought: "What am I to do in this place?" It was dark, but there were sensations of vibrations of light above and around. The message came to me: "Think about the mind in a new way." I wondered for a very long time how to do that, and eventually I thought of the other members of the seminar group, of their minds. I moved around the group; thinking about the nature of their individual minds and what we had done together. The music ended.

These are the messages I got:
Allow yourself to follow.
Throw away the ladder.
Think about the mind in a new way.

FIVE

Who Has the Power?

The Art of Becoming

In the Wood

The Rocket Ship

Contacting the Power Animal
Go to a favourite place in nature.
An animal will meet you there. Go with it!

16. Who Has the Power?

"Ohhhhhhh!"

I sense that I didn't quite make it in this journey.

On the first evening of the seminar, I took a walk. I walked for a bit, then I stopped, and I considered life and death in the forms of a living green pine tree and a burnt out, blackened, gorse bush. I walked around Life, prepared to be it, live it, do it. Then I looked at Death, and I decided to step right through the centre of the burnt bush as a symbolic death. When I stepped out the other side there was a major problem. Would I step back through and re-invent myself, or would I stay out there in limbo? But it seems I have learnt somewhere along the line recently that there are often three aspects to a choice, and the third aspect is not to make a choice. I walked off. After this, I considered myself dead and ready.

I chose to begin the journey to meet the power animal by standing at the burnt bush hoping to get direction, having decided not to rebirth myself; waiting there for the Coyote. Very strange incomprehensible things started to happen. A pale gold light shone, which could well be the power animal so I assumed that it was him. There was also the colour green, which I felt might be me. These colours were mixing together, twisting around each other and disappearing down a tunnel ...... (sigh) ...... I felt reluctant to struggle with incomprehensible stuff again.

Then my body split down the middle, revealing brown and green gashes like ploughed earth. An earthquake had raced through. One of the chasms caused by its passing ran down my left leg, and the coyote-ness went down following this trench. I noticed that other fractures went off in other directions. I wanted to point this out, to ask if it was important, but the coyote-ness was moving fast and I felt that I must follow him. We travelled along the chasm, trench, or rut, and went out of the bottom of the left foot. The crack ran on and on.

Ahead was a yellow sandstone cliff; a solid mass of rock stretching from side to side of my visual field and high into the sky. There were images visible on the rock face, I could see eyes and mouths but none of them connected to form complete faces. These half-perceived faces made the rock seem sentient and full of guardians. I thought: "The chasm must stop at the foot of this cliff." But the Coyote pushed on right through the rock, a very peculiar feeling.

On the other side there he was, about a foot tall, sat on my solar plexus. I was lying flat on my back and he was looking straight at me. He asked: "Who has the Power?" I replied swiftly: "I give it to you." It seemed right to say that in the context of what I am trying to do in my life, which is to be less fearful of consequences, to relax and find a different way to live.

We sank down into the darkness, the pitch black darkness. I wanted this. I became the darkness. I felt myself becoming the Black Coyote, and I announced: "I am my black self." It seemed to me that acknowledging this black self was a moment of power.

The other Coyote said: "Let's dance." Standing vertically, he danced on his back legs, and golden light, like spurts of molten ore, burst out of him. Golden bars twisted around each other and rolled up and down in the black space like pure energy. I couldn't dance like that; I couldn't even raise myself into the vertical. I had to dance lying down, and I danced a strange circling dance with a flat horizontal movement. It became a movement independent of my will and began to carry me, circularly, anticlockwise, essentially flat and horizontal, but with an undulation in the motion like a warped gramophone record, or the swell of the sea. I wondered if the wobble was caused by the earth as it settled down after the earthquake. When the dancing finished the Coyote disappeared and I was alone in blackness.

I stayed there for a while, looking and looking and seeing nothing. Then in the blackness I perceived a tarmac road. It was a neat trick to see the dark road in the darkness, but I didn't know anything. I didn't know whether to try to walk on the road, whether the road was laid on me, or whether I was the road. "What is going on?" I did nothing and kept on looking. I thought I saw a little ball of golden light. Again, I was wondering: "How far away is it? Is it moving towards me, am I moving towards it, is anything happening at all?"

Then the drumming changed, and the Coyote rushed me back to the beginning and we came through the journey again, slowly, slowly, trying to abstract more meaning out of each part, and arriving, eventually, at the same place.

When I shared this journey, Alexander asked me if I thought I answered the question right. Riddled with guilt, I said: "I didn't answer the question at all!" He said: "I think you gave the wrong answer. You should have taken your power. I think the Coyote wanted you to acknowledge your power." So now I have something to think about and meditate on. I will go and do that now.

I sat and meditated, and the Coyote clearly said to me: "Why don't you consider travelling in the body of the Owl to the lower world?" So I concentrated on preparing myself for that, and I experienced some very interesting and unexpected body sensations going along with it. Importantly, I found the answer to the question the Coyote asked me: "Who has the Power?" The answer I give him is: "We do."

> Journeying to the Lower World
> Meet your animal. Go through an entrance down into the lower world, look around, find a treasure.

17. The Art of Becoming

I got ready for this journey well in advance. I did this by sitting with the power objects that I had in my room and meditating on no thing, trying to empty myself in order to feel the bodiless spirit power. When the evening session started, I felt completely ready. I transformed my body into the body of the Owl during the first stage of the drumming. We were perched on the grey rock, a favourite place, and I felt very content. It was dark; on slow and silent wings, we took off and glided effortlessly down.

I saw yellow spots in the air, and I thought: "This is the colour yellow. Hum, I can't make much of it, but it is one of the medicine wheel colours." We observed it and I began to get used to this form of being. I was the Owl, but I was also schizophrenic in this way: the Owl would fly, and I would be flying as the Owl, but then I would say: "Whoa, stop, let's look at that again." So it was that I looked as long as I wanted at the yellow. Then I would make a request to move and onward we would fly again and we would enter the next experience, which was opaque white. This was more definitely a world, and we had a good look at it. Then we flew to the next world, which was black.

The blackness reminded me of the surface of dark water, and the Owl dived down and picked up a fish. This is a fishing Owl! I suspect that such birds do exist somewhere in the world. We had picked up a silver coloured fish, and I looked at it through Owl's eyes. It occurred to me that perhaps there were more. We took a net and we flew low, trawling the water. In the net we captured and pulled up glittering heaps of little silver fish. I threw them up out of the net into the sky where they became stars, and I thought: "Wah-heh! That was a gift for me! And I bet I can get a gift in every colour world."

So I determined to fly back to the beginning and get gifts from the yellow and from the white worlds. The way this was done was that in each world the Owl dived down and picked something up. Hidden in these worlds was everything that existed related to that particular colour. I couldn't see any of the things, all I could see was the colour, to me it was like a lucky dip, but I feel that the Owl knew what was there.

Down we went and up from the yellow world came a little golden house, like you would see on a charm bracelet. The silver fish was very similar to a charm as well. I began to think I was going to collect enough charms for a charm bracelet, how child-like and how charming.

We went to the white world. These worlds were cylindrical worlds that connected to one another as if they were descending sections of a stick; they were like bands of colour painted on a stick. In the white world, the Owl brought me a little white rabbit charm.

We returned to the black world, and I really wanted to play there and throw silver lights into the sky, but we already had our silver fish and I had a journey to make. We continued on into the red world where the Owl picked up a red ribbon. We-I-he-she threaded the three charms onto the red ribbon and tied a knot in it to make a necklace to put round our neck. The brilliant way the Owl could tie knots with its beak and its right foot as a hand, while its other foot was a foot for standing on, really impressed me. We tied an intricate knot in that red ribbon and then we wondered: "What to do now, now we have been through the colours?"

Now we had to go into the Unknown. It was fairly obvious that was what we had to do. I would have preferred to go and play in the blackness, but we pressed on through a barrier and we poked our head into an unknown universe. It was a closed sphere with a mechanical interior. I could see many pieces of charcoal coloured machinery, but none of them were moving and there was absolute silence. It wasn't a living universe. It was like a structure for a universe but without life. I thought: "Surely these colours of the medicine wheel can galvanise this place into life!" So I hit the colours with a sharp flap of my wings and the colour red flashed out, but the other colours didn't respond and it didn't work, nothing happened. I was at a bit of a loss.

In the silence, the spirit of the Great Owl spoke to me and said: "Surely enough of us have died for you to trust us completely?" So many species of Owl have come to me, alive and dead, that I had to admit this was the case. I didn't answer aloud; I expressed my trust by altering my mental state, allowing my brain function to change. For a while I thought I had failed because I seemed to come very close to normal consciousness and nothing happened. But I didn't panic, I just let my mind rest, and the Owl took me through another barrier into a pitch black place, or I went as the Owl, oh, you see, I don't know.

I looked into the blackness for a long time and adjusted to the new state. Ahead, at the end of a deep horizontal shaft-like tunnel, in an oval cleft, I spied a huge, black and terrifying-looking figure. He was shaped very like a human, but he was about forty feet tall and typically demonic. He was sitting on a throne of bare rock. He spoke, harshly, arrogantly, with disgust in his voice: "What are you doing here?" Cheerfully, confidently, even cockily, I said: "I have come for a look." I looked. The place was so black and so dark that I decided to show him the charms because I thought he might like the colours, maybe they would improve his mood. I took off the necklace and undid the knot. In front of me there was a parapet that was like a barrier indicating that I should not cross. I laid the charms out on this low flat-topped wall, from left to right: the golden house, the white rabbit, and the silver fish. I laid the red ribbon out too, placing it very carefully in a straight line above them. I said: "I'll give you these. I'll give you these in exchange for something." He fancied having them and he roared: "What do you want?" I said: "I want the colour green." I wanted the colour green to start my universe. In reply, he opened his mouth wide and I saw that the colour green was inside. He wanted those gifts, but he didn't want to give me anything, he was much too mean for that. He did not want to give me the colour green, so, how was I going to get it? In a flash I realized that the only part of him that had ever moved was his mouth. He was grown out of the rock and was totally immobile except for his mouth. Leaving the gift of the charms on the parapet, I flew up. I flew swiftly. I flew into his open mouth and snatched the Green. At that very second the drumming changed.

I remembered the entire journey with complete clarity, but I came back through every bit of it anyway, just for fun. I was pleased; I knew that with the colour green I could make that grey universe live. Ah, fantastic! Like a fairy tale! And that's where they come from, and that's where this came from, and that's where I come from, and that's what my power is all about! Whatever use is there to be for it in the way-we-do-it world I have no idea, but it feels good!

Taking a Trip to the Middle World
Go to an island. Meet your animal.
Go through a mist, see what happens.

18. In the Wood

I saw a landscape, rugged and wild. A shallow rock-strewn river ran through it. No boat could navigate those waters and there was no island. I saw a log stranded on the rocks. Perhaps it was a dugout canoe. But, no, it was a large piece of the trunk of a tree. Too curious I got trapped inside. A great flood came and swept the fallen tree down the river, leaving it high and dry on an island.

I was trapped inside. How could I possibly get out? I heard something, a loud knocking on the outside of the trunk; a Woodpecker was there, hammering his way into the wood. By his efforts he rapidly split the trunk and I was able to emerge. At the sight of me, the bright feathers of his red cap rose up in a magnificent display before slowly subsiding to their former sleekness. I thanked him profoundly for releasing me and decided to journey with him. We were about to fly off when I realised: "Wait a minute there's something wrong, we haven't done the mist." He dismissed the idea of mist, with a: "Pur-pher!" and the little mist that was knocking about, waiting for its opportunity, vanished in the face of his impatience.

Travelling fast, we headed in a northerly direction. I felt I must speak again: "Hold on, if we go too far north there won't be any trees for you to bore holes in." At the very edge of the tree line we landed. I had been flying behind him, and, all the way through the flight, I had been fascinated by the bright red cap on his head. Landing in this patch of vibrant colour, I rummaged around at the base of the red feathers where they enter the skin on the skull. I was thinking: "This is insane. What am I doing?" But my thoughts didn't stop me, and slowly I sank into the Woodpecker's head, then down into the body, where, unaccountably, the body of the Woodpecker became a tree and I was trapped again. I thought: "The only difference in this state to the one I was in previously is that I am now stuck vertically instead of horizontally. How am I going to get out now? Will I have to stay here for the rest of this journey?" It seemed a distinct possibility.

The Coyote arrived outside, and he shouted through the bark: "Make the tree flexible." It is totally unclear how but somehow this was accomplished and I was able to step down into the clearing and stand beside him. Then there was a long period when we did not move, where he showed me things and taught me things. What was he teaching? What was he doing? I can't remember: it's a blank. After a time, when he said: "Follow me" I found that I couldn't: I was stuck again.

Then, because I had lost it, he advised me, he wasn't exasperated, but, looking for the next step, he advised me to stay still, saying: "Well, you might as well relax and listen to the drum." I did, and the continuous second note that I have heard before became audible and became very, very important to me. As I listened to it, wondering how it was created, I began to rise up very slowly into a beautiful dark space. The feeling of rising was very, very nice, and I lay suspended in the dark space listening to the drumming. The Coyote told me to listen to it carefully, and, as I listened, I thought: "This will heal my heart, stop the arrhythmia, and make me feel happy." The Coyote said: "Listen to the drum bringing you the sounds of the future. Listen to the drum telling you what's coming in the future. Wait, wait, wait." He wanted to impress upon me that there is nothing more I need to do now but that, so I listened to the drum and let it affect my heart and a spiritual healing took place. I felt it spread over me. I could feel it working in my body. I felt very grateful that this was happening; I tried to be as pliable as possible and absorb it all.

I was extremely aware of the internal world of my body and the external world of the seminar. Outside the room a large, noisy skein of geese were approaching. I heard them coming, and I thought: "Oh, here's what the future is bringing. What are the geese saying? What do they mean?" And no insights came from it; they flew right by. A little while later, a second skein went over, even noisier, and I got a feeling that I was shielded lying in the black space. A feeling that there was a protecting wall around me; as if I was in a dark sanctuary; all that jostling, all that point and counterpoint, all those interrelationships that form the dynamics of a group; none of that could get in. That was good; it need not involve me.

As I lay thinking that it was ok for me to be out of it, uninvolved, a novel thing for me, another universe began to open up on my left-hand side. It was the most fabulous semi-transparent landscape of vertical drops into a deep blue sky and vertical cliff walls with luminous green plants and great trees growing on them, all illuminated by that especially clear and coolly brilliant, shining light. I have seen this place before; meditating after a perfectly ordinary walk on the Fell, re-walking the walk in my mind, I descended through the ground and discovered that this exotic and extraordinary nature world existed below. I looked down into it now. It opened from the space where I was, in the most soft way; a most inviting and seductive sensation of vertigo overtook me and I wanted to throw myself down into that fantastic world. I knew that I would not plummet down; I would float. And I knew that possibly all I could do was drift endlessly and observe. Nevertheless, it was infinitely fascinating to me and I wanted to go.

Suddenly I heard a banging under the floorboards by my left ear. The Coyote was knocking violently on the floorboards, but the noise wasn't in the journey it was happening in fact. The Coyote was calling me: "Come under the floor bones with me. I want you here, come under the floor bones." And I thought: "Oh damn! I don't want to go under the floorboards. What's under there? What's under there but dust and spiders?" The knocking got louder and eventually, because he was calling me, I did go through the wooden boards and under the floor.

Under-there opened out into a completely different landscape, more like a landscape from this world, more like some familiar countryside laid down to green pasture lightly dotted with trees. I was looking at it, wondering if it was as interesting as that fabulously otherworldly universe that I had wanted to vertigo myself into, when the drumming changed calling us to come back.

"Oh, I don't want to leave here now. And, not only do I not want to leave here, but I've no way of getting back without the Coyote." It had been so complicated: some of it was in visual pictures like a journey, some of it was spiritual healing, some of it was body shifts, some of it was here, some there, some nowhere, so I called him and he brought me back and I haven't lost much.

It was on the way back that a wind came up and disturbed the trees outside the room. I could hear them swishing and I thought: "Yes, by the power of the wind the trees are unstuck. That is how to make the tree flexible."

<u>Travelling to the Upper World</u>
Travel up a mountain with your animal.
Rise up through clouds. Go for it!

19. The Rocket Ship

Immediately the music started everything was black, beautiful, shiny black. I saw the tallest pitch black mountain with steep sides and a snow capped peak. Directly behind it a star shone brightly in the night sky, so that the star appeared to rest upon the top. I began to drift towards them, it was deep night and the sides of the mountain stretched up, merging into the sky, but that didn't daunt me. I was in a very happy state of mind and in the mood for some fun. I wanted to take all my totem creatures with me to the upper world and so I decided to call them.

The Black Coyote and the Yellow Coyote came at once, and then I called the others. I started in the root centre, and I called to the Rocks. I moved to the centre of generation, and I called to the Trees. I moved to the solar plexus, and I called the Owl. I moved to the heart centre, and I called the Deer. As they came, one after the other, I felt really proud.

When they were all present, I pointed to the star and said: "We are all going there. We will travel as a rocket; that is how we will travel." The Tree said: "I can make a rocket ship." The Tree would make the rocket ship out of its body. The Stones said: "With the energy which is locked into us, we will make the fuel to drive the rocket." The Owl offered to be the stabilisers. The Deer said: "With my horns, I will be the directional navigation system." The rocket ship began to take shape. The Black Coyote said: "I will be all the space that we have to travel through because I am the sum of all your incarnations so far and that makes the space that you have for your mind to play in." The Yellow Coyote would be the nose cone of the rocket, the part that gives it the inspiration to go.

We were ready to go and we went. But as we penetrated the outer atmosphere, which must be the required clouds, we realized that the stones had expended their energy in the launch, fragmenting their bodies to dust, and they were left behind. When we left the outer atmosphere, the rocket ship, which was the tree, fell apart and was left behind. I felt distraught that I had to leave these beloved things behind, but I was fierce with myself: "Keep it together!" We circled the Earth a few times and we looked down at it, blue and white. I said to the others: "Let's get it together. We have to go on now in the new vehicle that we have become."

This new vehicle was extremely strange. The horns of the Deer spiralled around each other and the colour black from the Black Coyote became one spiral while the colour yellow from the Yellow Coyote became the other spiral. The wings of the Owl remained to set our trajectory, and the two eyes of the Owl were stuck on the ends of the two spiral strands. They were my eyes, and that is how we travelled through the outer space-ness of it all.

Once the direction was set, it became clear that the brown wings of the Owl were no longer appropriate for the environment, and they fell off. Then there was just the double spiral; the black strand and the yellow strand, and the two eyes; yellow eyes with black centres, travelling through space; rolling, rolling through space with the spiral energy, beautifully orientated on the target, no problem at all.

We arrived at the top of the mountain and entered the star. After a little while spent getting used to this new environment, I realized that the star was an enormous faceted diamond. I could see some of the colours of the spectrum playing on the faces of this diamond, red, green and blue. I seemed to have lost my black and yellow spiral body; when I tried to visualize it, it didn't fit in that place at all. I knew I had achieved my goal and I entered a state of bliss.

But, all too soon, it was a bliss with an element of discontent because I felt purposeless and I thought: "Is this it? Is this what I sacrificed the trees and the stones for?" I didn't despair, I just thought: "Oh, is this all, to be inside a massive diamond in a state of suspended animation?" This diamond existence went on for quite a while. I thought: "I will just have to accept it. I integrated the two

Coyotes and this is where I ended up!"

Slowly, imperceptibly slowly, I became an oval-shaped bed of freshly dug brown earth located somewhere. A rainbow appeared. I was a flower bed, and I could grow those rainbow colours into flowers. Red, a single Tulip appeared. Orange, a Marigold sprang up. Yellow, a Buttercup flowered. Green, some Moss appeared. Blue: a Bluebell. Indigo, a Primula, and Violet was a Violet. That was very beautiful, very simple, very straightforward, and I felt fulfilled. With surprise I noticed that I was crying. I thought: "That's weird there are tears running out of my right eye, but am I sad?"

Suddenly a huge yellow eye was staring right at me. An Eagle, its head cocked on one side, its eye very close to the ground, was looking right at me. It struck into the ground with its beak and picked me up. As the Eagle swallowed me, I caught a glimpse of myself: I was an earthworm. The music stopped. Alexander said: "Come back." As I did come back horrendous, horrendous agony and utter misery hit me in waves on every single step of the journey, and those feelings got worse and worse.

SIX

Be Content with the Blue

Journey to the Inner Temple
Find inner healing and healing power.

20. Be Content with the Blue

My journey began in the morning when I was still at home. As I opened the front door and walked in and out, putting things in the car, a woman came past and following her a child leading a white pony. This child had red ribbons tying up her hair in bunches, and seeing her reminded me of a dream I had a few days previously.

I was walking through the streets of a busy city with a young child of five who was very shy and wouldn't join in the festivities that were happening there. We walked farther and, after a while, we came to a place where a group of children were getting ready to dance. My girl, who had grown and was now about ten, wanted to join in that dance, and I was very pleased that she seemed less shy.

As she danced, I was able to look at her closely and I noticed that she had red paint on her face, her forehead and cheeks were covered with bright red shapes made of straight lines. During the dance another girl, who was more experienced, did spiteful tricks like trying to trip her and push her out of the way. The lovely child didn't dance perfectly, but she danced beautifully, with feeling, and the actions of the spiteful child did not affect her at all.

When the dance was over she came back to me, and I congratulated her fervently: "I was so pleased that you joined in the dance." She replied: "Yes, I wasn't very friendly before because the people were strange to me and I didn't understand them, but now we have walked around for a bit and I have got used to them I can join in."

This dream was very touching and made a profound impression on me, so much so that just thinking of it causes me to weep. The red ribbons in the hair of the girl passing my door now brought it straight back to my mind. I watched them go past and left shortly after to attend the last day of a weekend seminar.

The music started and the journey began. I saw the girl with the red ribbons walking along the street. The pony had a blanket on which was cream coloured, with red and blue threads running through it making a grid pattern. I wondered where I fitted in. I was struggling to find my place in the picture, and, eventually, I was persuaded to see myself as the blue thread in the pattern of the pony's blanket. The pony and the girl had come to collect me, and becoming a thread in the blanket was the only way that I was able to travel with them that day.

We followed a road that ran gently uphill. My companions were innocent and pure, and everything was quiet, clear and divinely simple. We walked up onto a paved platform and went through an entrance between white stone pillars; we had entered a temple and it was blue sky. Amazed at the form that this temple took, I entered the blue, and, able to see more clearly now in the bright light, I looked and looked about me at the endless blue. After a while, a voice said: "Be content with the Blue." I was indeed questing for images, I stopped doing that and I became content with the blue.

After a long still period of quiet peace, I was taken into darkness, a darkness that contained the colour red. I saw a deep glow of red shining in the black, like hot coals in a banked-up fire.

I examined being in the darkness, and I examined being in the light; both were beautiful, comforting and filled me with awe, but the opportunities in each one were not at all similar, and I placed the different feelings that went with each of them into my memory.

Seeing then the colour green, I thought: "Oh, the journey is finished." I had time to ask myself: "How do you know that?" when the music stopped. In answer to my question, I would say that being in the green is being in a world of change, and that is my daily life.

In the final session of the seminar, when the sharing crystal came to me, I told this journey and I cried the whole way through. I cried because of the special blessing of simplicity.

SEVEN

Taken by the Eagle

The Many Grains of Sand

The Tourist

The Diamond Tip

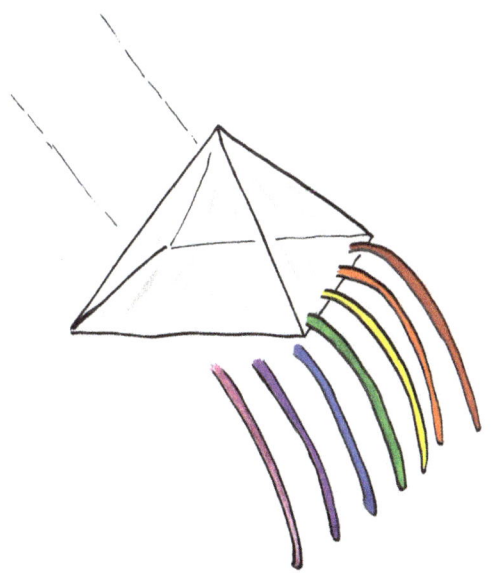

> Contacting the Power Animal
> Go to a favourite place in nature.
> An animal will meet you there. Go with it!

21. Taken by the Eagle

When the drumming started, I found myself standing in the dry river bed above the ominous deep dark pool by the cave of the Owl on the Fell. I decided to walk into the cave. Once inside I examined the limestone walls and the difference that being in there made to my consciousness. I felt myself changing. I decided: "I will become the Owl." I directed my energy to this. I felt myself lifting up, but, far from being the Owl taking flight, I was being lifted out of the rock by the Eagle who carried me up the course of the river bed like a piece of carrion. My body was hanging limply in the Eagle's talons like a dead rabbit.

I assumed: "I am dead." Then I thought: "No, I am not dead because I am still conscious." .... "Oh, the Eagle is going to drop me from a great height onto the rocks to break all the bones in my body to make me easier to eat." The Eagle didn't do that. I thought another thought: "The Eagle is going to fly to its nest and feed me to the Eaglets." But the Eagle didn't do that. It flew for a long, long time. Eventually we landed on a cliff ledge where there was a vertical golden crack. The Eagle pushed me into this crack with its beak. I got the feeling that the golden crack was an opening in the breast of the very Eagle that had carried me. I went through that crack; it was the entrance to the heart centre of the Eagle.

Within the crack I met the Coyotes. I took their hands in joy and relief and said with surprise: "I've found you here!" One was black and one was yellow, and something, that I can't quite remember now, was the colour white. Only the colour red was needed to make the medicine wheel. I determined to supply the colour red by becoming it.

The red was at the bottom and the white was at the top, the Black Coyote was to the right and the Yellow Coyote was to the left. It was not the medicine wheel as Joseph teaches it, Joseph, Teacher of mysteries, Alexander's Teacher and through Alexander, my Teacher. The wheel needed to be turned so that the Red was at the top in the North, Yellow in the East, White in the South and

Black in the West. I couldn't work out exactly how to make it right, so I just let it happen and, by various means of twisting and turning, it was achieved. There was the medicine wheel as Joseph teaches it.

The wheel began to spin. Then it fractured. I saw the black, the yellow, and the red fly away like jagged lightning flashes. I was left alone with the colour white. I stood in the white space waiting.

A young woman approached me who was dressed all in white. She came close, then turned and began to walk away. I called to the two Coyotes: "I am going to leave you here. Make yourselves into a gate, and if I ever return, I will come back through this gate." I turned and followed the White Woman. As we walked, I asked her a question: "How can I walk straight?" I asked this because earlier in the day I couldn't walk straight. The seminar group took a meditative walk to the beach to understand the art of walking and, when we arrived, we sought a blessing from the ocean. When I walked down to the sea, I was staggering all over the place. The Coyote shouted at me: "Walk in a straight line!" This helped me pull myself together and, when I concentrated hard, I did manage to walk straight. That is why I asked the woman: "Teach me to walk in a straight line."

She danced a very strange dance, a shuffling dance where the steps seemed to move backwards while she went forwards. Her head was down, her body leaned slightly forward, her arms were held straight but pointing to the ground behind her. It was a concentrate-on-the-ground dance. Step forward with the right foot to touch the ground with the toes, then pull the foot backwards and place it half way along the left foot so that the heel of the right foot rests in the instep of the left foot. Take a similar step with the left foot. Then repeat this step with the right foot, but instead of putting weight on it as it rests on the ground by the instep of the left foot, drag it back farther along the ground so that both feet are level. Pause and stand for one moment, and then step forward with the left foot and, leading with this step by the left foot, start the sequence again. That's the dance she taught me.

Then she melted away and a white horse appeared. I tried, not for the first time, to trust this horse and to get onto its back. After a struggle I succeeded, I was up riding on the back of the horse and we were travelling in the colour white. I looked up and I saw blue sky above. White eagles were circling, several of them, and a clear yellow sunlight shone. My spirits rose.

The drumming changed and I came back. I lost a few things. I don't remember what form the colour white from the medicine wheel took on, and I don't remember some other things. For example, some body changes, like when I became the colour red I have a feeling that I became very tall and thin. But I have managed to record the essence of the journey.

Well, after I had made that recording I remembered how the medicine wheel colours worked. It was like this: I went forward with the Coyotes, the black and the yellow, on either side. Ahead was the white, into which we walked, and there was the White Buffalo. I saw the White Buffalo in the space inside the Eagle and that is how the colour white came into the medicine wheel. Then the only colour that was left to find was the red and I took on that colour at that time, so the mystery about who supplied the form for the colour white is solved.

> Journeying to the Lower World
> Meet your animal. Go through an entrance down into the lower world, look around, find a treasure.

22. The Many Grains of Sand

My body was lying on the seminar room floor relaxing before the journey. I felt very calm and still, the Owl enveloped me, and I stood on the stone I had brought with me from the entrance to the fairy kingdom on the Fell, a favourite place.

The drumming started. The Black Coyote appeared like a whirlwind and knocked me sideways, off the stone and out of my body to the left. Although it took me completely by surprise, I accepted his tornado arrival and he took me down through a series of vortices which were on the left-hand side of my body; one, two, three, vertically down, and then along a more horizontal one that cut into my body and made all of my lower centres jump.

We went into complete blackness, travelling together very

closely, with him leading the way. It was a long dark journey during which I experienced physical ecstasy. I found I could do amazing things with my body. I could open it up and see and feel the thousands of folds that went right the way down the front, all billowing and flapping like fronds of tall seaweed in the darkness of the blackness, layers upon layers unfolding to be felt and seen.

After a long while, we came to a world where some blue circular patterns were visible on the ground. When I bent down in the gloom to have a close look I found that these were black pebbles, some very small amount of light was reflecting off them and that is how they appeared to be blue. Still crouching down I looked along the beach, the scene was familiar, and I felt sure I had once met the girl and the horse here. I looked up and there they were, standing by a large rock. Moving ahead of the Coyote I went towards them. Coming up to the girl, I stepped into her and we became as one person. We travelled and we entered a sandy desert that was flat for as far as the eye could see.

We looked around; there wasn't much to see. A conference followed, between the three of us, White Horse, Girl with Red Ribbons and Black Coyote, because something was missing. It was a something with the quality of yellowness. We decided we would look for this yellowness and we wanted to find a golden-yellow sphere. We knew the size of sphere we were searching for, the diameter of which would have been from the level of my eyes to my navel. The three of us stood in a circle and we wondered how we could find anything in this desert where there was nothing but sand. I expected one of us to have the answer, but it became an endless think-tank of how to proceed. Going round and round in circles, the discussion lasted for aeons. We were stuck in an endless loop. We were completely stuck.

So, faced with complete inability to achieve the goal we had set ourselves, we began to compromise and we said: "Yes, so, well, ok then, this sand is made of millions of golden-yellow spheres, so let's choose one of those." .... But which one? How to make a choice? And this became even more distressing because there were billions and billions of grains of sand and in what way would you choose between one and the other? And how would you ever construct a system to find the one that you wanted? How would you ever know it was the right one? We were overcome by choice and another state of extraordinary stuck-ness took over, only very slightly different to the one before.

I thought hard, because this sphere was a symbol in my meditative life that belonged to somebody important: "Who was it that owned a golden sphere?" After a long struggle, I remembered that the golden sphere belonged to the Yellow Coyote. As soon as I had that thought the Yellow Coyote erupted out of the sand like a dust devil. Creating his own vortex, many grains of sand were attracted to him as he rose from the desert floor and many grains of sand were falling from him as he shook his body into shape. He shouted at us, not in anger, more in exasperation, and he said: "What does it matter if it is one grain or a million? I can make myself out of any grain here, or I can choose a thousand grains of sand, or a million, and I can make myself out of all these grains of sand into any size I want." And he began to grow, and grow, and grow, and that was magnificent to watch. I mean, I would have been quite happy if for the rest of the journey the Coyote had just grown out of the vast desert into the hugest, hugest, hugest creature that I had ever seen. But suddenly he vanished.

We were deserted, left looking at each other in a helpless kind of way. Less than helpful thoughts came my way and I looked impatiently at my companions thinking loudly to myself: "That white horse is completely redundant. I can't even imagine what it is doing here." Then I asked the girl: "What shall we do?" and she hopped from one foot to the other, like a little bird dancing. It was a pretty pathetic dance. It was quite obvious that it would achieve nothing, so, ignoring the Black Coyote, I said emphatically: "This place is finished. Let's go back to the place that we came from."

We retraced our steps and came to the black pebbles, I turned to the Black Coyote and I affirmed that I trusted him completely and that I understood that I would be with him while he was teaching me something that was extremely hard, and that I would try my best to depend upon him. I said: "You allowed me to follow that phantasy, so that I could learn from it. I know it is a lesson about the nature of time and choice. How points of time are like a desert of sand and there is no choice to be made between one or another point of time, or any difference between them. That the greatest thing I can do or achieve is either in one point in time or a million and I have got those millions of points of time. But why make a choice and how would that choice be made? So" I said, drawing breath: "if that is the lesson there, I will follow you now." And he said: "Yes, follow me." In fact, after I had said all that I think he smiled at me encouragingly and said: "Well, now follow me."

We entered into complete darkness. Darkness without vortices, darkness without feelings, darkness without movement, without excitement, without a sense of purpose, and I began to get suffocated. I thought: "I am starting to panic." I asked the Black Coyote to come closer to me because I trusted him and he was all I had. My breathing was eased by bringing him closer and, after a moment, I found that the back of my body was opening up just like the cargo doors on the bottom of an aeroplane. As we exited through my open back the suffocating feeling stopped and we entered a place that was formless; there was no pressure either, it was a no-thing place, and that is where we stayed. I listened to the drum, which held me together; otherwise I would have fallen apart.

When the drumming changed to call us back I depended entirely on the Coyote because I could not have returned. The Black Coyote brought me back and, on the way, I saw that sterile desert that only the Yellow Coyote could make sensible, it looked like an off-shoot of a root, or, perhaps, the appendix.

We were nearly back when I remarked anxiously: "What happened to the vortices on the way back?" The Coyote laughed and said: "The vortices are only on the way down. Your consciousness has changed and you won't go back through them unless you returned to the same place which you won't do."

We came back and I came out of that trip as fast as I could. I had no desire to re-live or dwell in any of it, but I knew perfectly well that it was engraved in my memory in such a way that I wouldn't forget it. The experiences, in the blackness and the darkness, of the strange capabilities of my body have not diminished, but what can they mean to me? Luckily, to some extent, the unbearable intensities of the difficulties in the sand desert have gone. Yes, and some of the overwhelming feeling of the no-thing-ness has also gone. But I felt very serious and silent and detached when I came back. Someone in the group asked a question. That brought me back to life and I saw this world as quite a treasured place to be because it has infinite variety in it and all the parts of it seemed to me like precious dinky toys.

> Taking a Trip to the Middle World
> Go to an island. Meet your animal.
> Go through a mist, see what happens.

23. The Tourist

Alexander made a specific suggestion for this middle world journey. He suggested that we go to the fairy worlds, so I went to my room to get the stone that I had brought with me from the entrance to the fairy realms on the Fell. I put it on the medicine cloth. It sat there looking very big, although it is only about the size of a round loaf of bread.

The drumming started and I saw the White Horse standing on a beach by a foaming sea; no wonder the horse had been so useless in the desert. Shaking her snowy mane, she whinnied a greeting. In the cool air steam came swirling from her nostrils while the white water waves cascaded onto the shore around her legs and these two things together created the mist. My hand on her shoulder, we walked along the shoreline, the horse with her hooves in the sea and myself, to the left, on the sand.

By the way, I knew that we were in Ireland. In my mind, I see the map of Ireland from the air and a certain part to the north west takes my attention. When I look in the atlas that area is Donegal, maybe this was Donegal Bay.

The horse turned seawards and waded into the surf; I waded alongside her. Then, putting my arms around her neck and one leg over her back, I hung there on the left-hand side. When we got into the deep waters, the Coyotes came as two curious seals, dogs of the sea. I thought with some surprise: "This is amazing because I don't like swimming in the sea and getting wet, but I feel perfectly happy now."

I pulled myself up onto the back of the horse and we were in another place, no longer under the water but on dry land. The Coyotes came out of the next wall of wave and, as they emerged, they changed from seals to hounds. They became beautiful grey coursing hounds with long legs and elegant curving backs, with lithe bodies and slim curling tails. They were my hunting dogs and I adored them. The White Horse was my horse, strong and swift. I looked at myself: I was a man, I had a shield, I had a spear and this felt so good. We began to hunt and the feeling was powerful and enlivening. We chased a great wild razorback boar; we chased him through forests and we chased him across moors. The hounds danced with their jaws dripping with blood. They danced in the sky and they danced on the ground. They danced the dance of the dying animal as danced by the predator, the ritual killing dance, and it was fulfilment, it was brilliant.

But, in fact, there was no killing of this Boar. He led us instead to the gates of a castle with many turrets and towers. I knocked loudly at the gate and shouted: "Let us in!" The gate opened and my self and my animals went in. Leaving them in the courtyard, I came into a great hall where a feast was laid out. The tables were arranged to form a semicircle and the floor was of beaten earth. I thought: "This must be a fairy place because there are no people and yet the food is magically ready." So I brought the animals into the hall for company and sat down. As I ate, the White Horse, which was standing in the centre of the open space, transformed into a beautiful woman. I fell in love with her and she took me upstairs to a turret room where was her bed which was herself. Her skin was pure white and the bed was made with fresh white sheets, beautiful to look at and comfortable to lie in. I could look out of the turret window at the panoramic view of the forest, enjoy it and feel totally protected.

I stayed there for a long time until one day I said to her: "This isn't enough for me. I miss the hunt. My dogs miss the hunt. We need to go. We need to do that challenging thing that we enjoy.

We need the red blood." I continued: "I need my horse. Please become my horse again." The white bed, because I have to say that it was more of a bed than a woman, became the white horse again. I spoke to the horse: "The trouble is that being white you are not great as a hunting horse; you show up too much against the landscape." Willingly the horse transformed, becoming a black horse, and we left the castle.

We searched and we found our quarry, a female wild pig, a sow. We found her lying in a thicket suckling piglets that were still in those lovely stripped coats of chestnut and honey brown. I counted the piglets and there were five. I said to the hounds: "It seems a pity to kill this sow and destroy these piglets, so let's not do that." And we sat down to enjoy watching them grow.

I picked one up and I thought: "Shall I just take one, for a pet?" And I decided: "No." So it was that in this way we became protectors and guardians of the piglets and when they were grown I sent them out in five directions. I wondered: "What they will do? Can I predict what they will do? I can't, because they are powerful animals and they do what they want. They may do anything and I cannot know what it will be."

The Piglets were gone and I thought: "I will look more closely at the Sow. Perhaps there is something more that I can learn or see." As I looked I was very surprised to see her turn into a black panther, which addressed me, saying: "Follow me." Willingly I turned to mount the horse to find another surprise; she had changed again into black and white, the colours of shade and light, changed into a piebald horse, a pinto pony, perfect camouflage. Joyfully, I leapt upon her back. I called the hounds to me and we journeyed following the Black Panther through the woodland wild.

She brought us to a clearing where there was an extremely strange Being. I tried to call it by a name and I thought it might be an Elf, but it didn't coincide with the pictures I have seen of Elves, it seemed built out of the landscape, more like a wind and water eroded stone, more like the remnants of a moss-covered tree. It was perched up on a mound, and it was not clear where the mound ended and the Being began. I had the impression that it was up there so that I could not reach out and touch it.

Casually it spoke: "You got here then." The sound of the voice informed me that 'it' was a 'he'. I replied: "Yes, bit of a miracle isn't it?" Silence. He was not a convivial and I knew he would say nothing unless I initiated the conversation, but it was quite difficult to know what to say. I wracked my brain for interesting topics. I only remember the answer to one particular question. I asked: "How many alternative realms of existence are there?" And he said: "Oh, eight hundred thousand ...." he paused meaningfully, looked at me mysteriously, and added: "...... or more." I quipped: "There's not really time to make a map then, is there?" I saw myself as an other-worlds' tourist, going to look and coming away, contributing nothing. I thought: "That is really rather what I am doing here. Because what am I doing here?"

I looked around at the place. It held a hypnotic fascination for me, but, resisting that, I turned to the Being and I said: "The thing is that I am supposed to be finding out more about my relationship with this horse. And, now I have travelled so happily with it, I think I had better go back through the journey to see if I can learn anything more before I lose it all." So I whistled the coyote-hounds and they came running in from where they had been hunting. Each one was carrying a hare; they dropped them at my feet and the hares jumped up and sprang away. They looked so beautiful and energetic as they leapt effortlessly through the landscape.

We began to travel back. On the way back, I would ask the Coyotes who were running alongside the horse: "What happened next?" And a little further on: "What happened next?" And again: "What happened before this?" and through them I would remember. Eventually we came back. I think I was at the stage where I was first riding the white horse and, looking at my spear and my shield, finding my man-nature, when the drumming changed for the return. I did the final return through the water during the fast drum beats, came back and lay deeply enjoying all the graphic imagery of that terrific trip, so I deeply thank the fairy stone for its assistance this evening.

Travelling to the Upper World
Travel up a mountain with your animal.
Rise up through clouds. Go for it!

24. The Diamond Tip

The drumming started and I was standing on this Earth, thinking: "Oh dear!" I had absolutely nothing in my mind. Like a bolt of lightning, the Eagle came, snatched me up, flew me straight to the top of the black mountain and dropped me in front of the diamond at its tip. I thought: "Oh, I am here again." Then I panicked, I could see no way in, and I realized: "No power animals with me!" I started to look around for animals when I heard the echo of the Coyote's laughter, he said: "You'll have to knock to get in this time."

I knocked on the diamond and a very strange thing happened, it shot away taking me with it and with it also went the blackness of the mountain so that the mountainside opened up. The diamond flew to the north, then it flew to the west and opened up all of that side, then it flew to the east and flew to the south like a ball on a pin-ball machine. It was like a centrifuge of the sort in which they train astronauts, except that I was the one in the diamond as it flew around and across. Then it seemed to spin around a couple of times and I found myself at the centre of a vast black bowl standing on a platform that rose from the middle of the bowl as if they were one piece of moulded plastic. Next to me on this platform was the, now much smaller, multi-faceted diamond.

I looked around. At the periphery of the bowl, a few small diamonds were visible, like chippings off the one that had ricocheted around and opened up the mountain. I looked up at the dark sky above. The power animals were all playing above me, like the aurora borealis, their many coloured and fluid forms were flickering across the sky. I wondered if I should reach up and grab one. Should I wait until the horse passed over and grab the horse? "Ah-hah!" I realized suddenly: "I know what to do." I picked up the diamond and, pressing it against my forehead, I pushed it straight into the eye centre.

Immediately I was back in the seminar room looking at all the people lying there. I looked around at the bodies and the memory of the healing power of crystals came to me; I went to each person with healing intent. Then I came and stood beside Alexander drumming, and I thought: "I wonder if he could know that I was here?" After a while standing next to him enjoying the experience, I noticed that it was possible to go into the drum. I went through the skin of the drum and I became a pebble, rolling and rolling and rolling around inside the drum making a rattling sound. A voice asked me: "What do you want?" The question was big: "What do you want in your life?" I had to think very carefully because everything that came to me quickly soon seemed banal, crass and pointless. Finally I said: "I want to dance."

I was thrown upwards and I became a star alongside many other shining silver points in the night sky, and we hung there. As the drumstick hit the drum, the stars would shake and jump. This came to me: "All stars twinkle, don't they? That is the stars dancing." It was very beautiful. The face of the Coyote appeared in the sky. His smile extended the length of the Milky Way. I was one of the stars in the smile of the Coyote. I was a smile, or, to be more accurate, a part of a smile. Enlivened by a feeling of happiness I was aware of a certain obligation to journey on. I retraced my steps and when I came to the beginning I walked around the journeying people again. Then I stood beside Alexander and the drum beat changed for us all to come back.

EIGHT

Getting Up the Elephant's Nose

The Ascending Spiral

The Way to the Stars

<u>Contacting the Power Animal</u>
Go to a favourite place in nature.
An animal will meet you there. Go with it!

25. Getting Up the Elephant's Nose

As Alexander was talking to the group before the journey started, I began to see very clearly the internal surface of an elephant's trunk. I soon realized that I was standing inside an elephant's nose at the top of its trunk. The trunk was like a water shute formed from grey rock and I was sure that at the bottom of this shute there was a beautiful pool. When I exited the elephant's trunk, I would drop into this pool and see that I had just come down a beautiful waterfall. There would be a lovely sandy shore to sit on and beautiful nature all around. I thought: "That is good, maybe I will meet the Coyotes down there."

But suddenly the Coyotes were at the top of the trunk with me. They were in a very peculiar form, like cardboard cut-outs and small, standing on their hind legs they only reached up to between my knees and my waist. They were both there, identical, except that one was yellow and one was black. I politely said hello to them, but they weren't so terribly keen to be sociable. Swiftly we decided to form a boat so that when the water would gush through, which would happen when the drumming started, we would fly down the waterfall as a boat and drop into the pool. So we sat: the black one at the front as the prow, I decided that would be good as he was the past, the yellow one behind me, as he is the future. I felt very pleased with this arrangement. It was quite logical: I can see my past but I can't see my future.

When the drumming started there was no water, not even one trickle. I looked around, the cave we were in was formed by the skull of the elephant, and I could see two portals above us, which were the eye sockets. In front of us, I noticed that the shute had a ridge of stone in the middle, making it more like two shutes side by side. While I waited for the rush, I speculated which route the boat would take.

Not a speck of water came and we just sat there. After a while, the Coyotes decided what a good idea it would be to tickle the nasal passage of the elephant with the Yellow Coyote's tail. This would make it sneeze and this would blow us out of the nose. I strongly disagreed: "No! Don't do that because if you get up you will destroy the boat and then we will get separated in the downward blast and maybe we won't find each other again."

But it was too late; they both got out and dis-formed the boat. The yellow one took hold of his own tail and tickled the upper nose of the stone elephant. We were shot forward by a great rush of air and water mixed and we plopped into a pool. I was very pleased to find that they were still with me, but, instead of landing in the beautiful nature pool, we were sitting in the grey, muddy water of a shallow circular depression. All the land around this waterhole was the same mud-grey colour. At a little distance, the surface was rough, dry and cracked, but it was smooth and slippery around the edges of the pool where the water had splashed onto it. I was deeply disappointed. I thought: "This is hideous."

In an upbeat way, the Coyote asked me: "What do you think of the colour grey?" I replied mournfully: "I have always hated the colour grey. Everything is the same." He said: "No, everything isn't the same. Everything is grey, but everything isn't the same. Feel the water." I did, and yes, the water was fluid and I absorbed all the feelings of the water. He said: "Now climb out of the pool and feel the ground." Yes, it did feel very different. He was right: the fact that they were all grey had nothing to do with same-ness.

Then it began to dawn on me that we might still be inside the elephant. Before I had time to decide if we had been sucked in and not blown out at all, the Coyotes turned into two of those hoppers that children bounce around on. One was a black hopper and one was a yellow hopper. Their ears became the two things to hang onto and they wobbled and bounced around this grey world. The sight was very amusing, but, at the same time, I wasn't unreservedly humorous about it. I thought despairingly: "This elephant has turned into a bouncy castle and the whole journey has become completely childish. Yes, it is sweet, and it is funny, and all that, but, well, is this it?" Anyway, they wouldn't stop bouncing so perhaps I should join in. I thought it through: "If I choose one of them to ride on I might upset the other one. So, no, I can't sit on one and bounce about and I certainly can't sit astride both of them at once and bounce, so I am going to have to become one myself." I became a grey hopper and we all bounced, boing, boing, boing.

We bounced right out of the cave of the elephant. It reminded me of jumping out of the pouch of a kangaroo and, not surprisingly, the Coyotes turned into kangaroos: we had jumped into Australia. We were high on an escarpment. The grey elephant, or cave in the rock face, or whatever we had just come out of, was behind us. The ground ran down and away into the biggest plain that I have ever seen. I could never ever see the end of this plain which was dotted with trees and scrub and there were signs that many animals browsed upon it.

The coyote-kangaroos were ready for the off, but I hesitated: "We can't just go out there. We will get lost. We will never find our way back here." They were highly amused by this and they said: "Was it so brilliant inside the elephant's nose that you want to find your way back?" Recalling the guidelines, I said: "No, but it is where, you know, we came from there so we should come back there." They replied: "Well, is that a beginning? Where were you before you were in the elements' nose?" Elements' nose! Didn't they mean elephant's nose? I confessed: "I don't know where I was before that." They said, triumphantly: "You see, you don't know, you've forgotten. So you can't go back to where you came from anyway. We don't know what your problem is."

There was a long moment when we did not move from the environs of that cave. Then, I think they slightly tricked me because they know I love to fly, they became bird's wings and I became the body and we flew. I think it was partly a trick and partly that, on reflection, I realized that I didn't know where I had come from before the cave and so, what was my attachment to it? And, beyond the journey instructions, what was my obsession with going back to where I came from?

The flying was really good fun. Our composite bird-creature was very strange; it had a black wing, a yellow wing and, as the body of it, I, no longer grey, was also black. The endless landscape became more and more geometric, until, ahead of us, the only vista was two horizontal straight lines with a tiny gap between them; we flew through that gap into geometry.

I felt the Coyotes lag behind, and I found myself pressed up against what seemed to me to be a large pearl; it was white and iridescent. There was no space behind me, just a black wall, and the front of me was pressed against the sphere of the pearl as if I was pressed against a window. I thought: "The only thing to do is go forwards." I went into the pearl-like sphere. In the centre I found a black dot, at first it reminded me of the black blob in an individual egg of frogs' spawn, and then it reminded me of the black hole at the centre of an eye.

I thought: "Oh, I will go into the centre of the darkness." I went in. It was brilliant, brilliant in there, and I heard the Coyote say: "This is the place of lost beginnings." Eagerly searching for those beginnings, I looked and looked, and it seemed to me that this black centre was full of little golden threads. They were all about half the length of my body. I remembered that when we were outside the cave I had wanted to have something like a string by which I could return to the point of origin, like an Ariadne's thread, but nothing was available there. Here, where all these fibres were, I could tie them all together and make a really long rope, so that, when I left the place of lost beginnings, I could have this rope with me and by unravelling it as I went along I would always be able to find my way back. Surely the place where I came from must be somewhere here.

I began to tie all the threads together and I wondered: "Is this the gift the Coyotes are giving me? It may be." It is always good to exchange gifts and I thought on: "I would like to give them a gift." Meantime this enormous hank of rope was getting bigger and bigger and bigger. The only way that I could look after it was to wind it round and round my body until it became like a dress. Then, as I wound on, I thought: "No, perhaps it is not the gift; the Coyotes are telling me something. They have been dropping big hints that my sense of humour isn't up to much and that I have got a bit too serious and heavy, but, still, I would like to give them a gift. There isn't much here, but I am tying a lot of knots and I think if I tie their tails together that would be funny, wouldn't it? A gift of a joke: that would be funny." So, in the darkness, I did tie their tails together and I imagined what it would be like when they found out that they had been tied up. Imagining this was a mistake: I fell into mental anguish because I don't ever want anybody to be hurt. I thought: "Oh, is this a nice joke? Is it funny?" Personally, I hate practical jokes. "Is it funny, or, when they pull apart, will it be painful and they won't be able to get undone? Is it spiteful?" I was in the middle of worrying about it when the drumming changed and, horror struck, I shouted: "Oh no, we've got to go back!" The Coyotes came on either side of me. With their knotted tails they scooped me up between them as if they had put me in a basket and we shot back at high speed to the nose of the elephant.

I lay there and went through all the journey again. Yes, they laughed at me, they tricked me, they messed me about the entire time, and I never wanted to leave them because I love them more than my own life.

Journey to the Inner Temple
Find inner healing and healing power.

26. The Ascending Spiral

Alexander sprang this journey on us unexpectedly and that just shows how brilliant he is. We took this journey to music. I didn't listen to what he was saying as he talked us into the journey. Instead, I found myself walking towards and entering into a very large tree, entering into the golden space that exists within the tree. In the centre of this tree-space there was a nodule on the ground, something like what I imagine the pituitary gland to look like; it looked like a little mushroom, or like a table-shaped internal growth of the wood of the tree growing up from the ground like a platform. I knelt and put my forehead on this platform in an attitude of praying. I was quite happy if I simply stayed there for the entire journey because the visual intensity of the brown tree and the goldenness within was so pleasing.

But when the music started the Coyotes came and began to dance in a very stately way around the circular space where I knelt in the middle. I looked up and they became two spiralling columns, shining black and translucent yellow. Then, as they slowly rose in twisting, curling columns of light, I saw the colour pink appear and turn with them, then the colour blue and then green, so that there were five columns of translucent light turning like smoke and rising upwards. I found that I was rising with them. The most overwhelming sensation of joy came into me; my stomach began to bounce, my rib cage began to heave, and I wanted to cry out loudly under the intensity of this agonisingly beautiful experience of rising in the columns of light. I became so intensely emotional that I thought I couldn't go on. I had lost sight of the Coyotes. I cried out to them: "Where are you?" and they said: "We are making this tree for you. Don't worry, we are still here, we are making this tree."

The overpowering feeling diminished and I began to see a bowl made of blue and yellow petals with crystal-like quality. I was resting in the centre of this bowl. The bowl began to turn, very slowly, anticlockwise and move off to the left. As it moved, it closed over me and the colours changed from blue and yellow to black and yellow. I was held within this black and yellow ball. It moved out and up to the left and I was able to see the entire shape and structure of the tree, the branches radiated out from the trunk in a great circling, clockwise sweep. A shape like the image of a galaxy was formed as the branches grew out and upwards to the sky.

The black and yellow ball took me outside the periphery of the tree to circle in orbit. I was held within the ball, but I was conscious outside of it and from outside I watched. I saw the arms and legs and tails and snouts of different animals emerge from the ball. I saw the arms and feet of a kangaroo. Then I saw the hands and feet of a shrew-like creature, its nose and tail also peeped out. These images continued and I could have stayed and watched as every single four-limbed creature emerged in part from this sphere and then disappeared into it again.

I thought about the journey and I wondered: "What is the purpose of it?" I began again to feel agony, of a different sort to ascending the spirals of light, the agony of a painless but pointless existence. I felt this more and more, so I looked down again towards the tree. In the space created above the crown, I could see big birds circling. I looked into the centre of the vortex there and I could see that the coloured columns of light travelling up the trunk of the tree were coming out of the top in a great rising spiral, creating thermals for these enormous birds to soar upon. I came into the consciousness of one of these birds, a most gigantic Condor. It was circling without effort, higher and higher and higher, on the heat from the centre of the tree. I looked down and I saw the other birds far below. I circled up, up, up on the thermal column, way, way, way beyond any images.

Then I saw a great hand that was closed into a fist. The closed fingers were the columns of gigantic stone cliffs. I flew towards the vertical faces of these cliffs. There was no ledge for a bird to land. Gliding with the cliffs to my right I noticed that streamers of wispy cloud were floating on my left-hand side. I flew into these clouds. As I flew on, I became more and more wispy myself until I lost consciousness of the form of the bird and became cirrus cloud. I wondered: "What is this for?" but without any joy, or agony, or any feeling now. I debated with myself what I could do, because I kept looking back and farther and farther away was the tree and the world. I formed a plan. I thought that I could condense as rain and fall upon the earth, but my heart wasn't into doing that.

As I was thinking: "No, I don't want to descend, however altruistic that might be." I happened to glance up and I saw that the Condor was above, flying higher, still higher. I saw that the two Coyotes were in the Condor and I went up to join them. We went higher. When we reached a certain height an immense Spiritual feeling entered my body; it had no form, no image and no colour, nothing but a feeling. It came into me further and further and further and I just kept staying with it, holding onto it.

The music came to an end and in no way did I want to return, but eventually the two Coyotes did tug at me and I turned my attention to them. They condensed themselves into a ball around me again and, in this way, we came back without too much agony. As we travelled back, we looked at the places we had been on the way out. When it came to where the animal forms were coming out of the black and yellow ball as it circled the tree I noticed again that the ball of forms was orbiting anticlockwise. I wondered if we ought to travel back through it in a clockwise direction, but, in fact, if that had been possible it would have caused a tremendous disaster. We circled anticlockwise, as before, and returned in good order. That holds my attention: we could not travel through the motion of the circle in the opposite direction to the flow. So, even though the instructions make it clear that the traveller should return along the same route, the guidelines don't apply in circular motion where there is no beginning or end. And I saw that the motion of the upward rising spiral is different, in that, it does have a beginning and an end.

When we return to the place of the ecstasy of travelling in the rising columns of light the Coyotes bent the rules again and brought me down the outside of the spiral so that I was able to observe the colours, but I did not enter the overwhelming feeling that I had experienced on rising. As I descended, I noticed that the light decreased in jumps and that, on each level of the descent, the light was markedly less intense.

Next Steps Journey
Use your imagination!

27. The Way to the Stars

We came to take our next steps journey. I felt that I would like to begin from the place where the previous journey finished with the nameless force inflowing, but, of course, I couldn't just turn that on.

When the music for the journey started, I was quietly held immobile. A flight of wide shallow steps led downwards through the centre of my abdomen and that was the direction that I should go if this was my next steps journey, and was it? There were steps, it was a journey, and it was down into the dark beauty within the Void. I thought: "Well, I had better do that another time because Alexander instructed us to travel upwards." I was also reluctant to travel this sacred downward journey and then share it with the other people on the course. There were some difficult customers among them and it had not been an easy week. If I took it, I must share it, no doubt about that.

I called the Coyotes to help me go up. They came into my hands as two oblong blocks. I moulded them into two star-shoes. These had a particular shape and looked something like spearheads. I put them on and I began to climb the soft dark mountains of the sky. It was like climbing in soft black sand. It was quite a different sensation to a flight of stairs, it was hard work and I seemed to sink backwards on every step that I took, but I climbed and climbed and climbed. Nothing very much happened. I could see the vast expanse of black space dotted with distant stars. The air was crystal clear and empty yet, at the same time, there was a soft sinking-ness to the space.

Then a Spiritual presence came and stood behind me, putting hands on either side of my body and pressing these hands against me, and I stopped climbing. I stood still with this Being. I listened to the music and I became certain notes in the music. Then I became extremely still and calm and attentive and empty, and I stayed there for the longest time, even after the journey was finished.

In the period when other people were writing their notes Alexander put some music on again quietly. I found that my spirit body was shifting. I felt one or two quite radical movements. It seemed to me that was something I might be going to do next: travel in my spirit body in a new way.

NINE

In the Eagle's Body

The Green Marsh

Through the Spirit Lodge

> Journeying to the Lower World
> Meet your animal. Go through an entrance down into the lower world, look around, find a treasure.

28. In the Eagle's Body

I need to say something about the instructions that Alexander gave us for this journey. He said that we should go to a beautiful place in nature; call the power animal and exchange gifts there. Then he said that we would journey with this animal to find something that we had lost, something that we had lost in our childhood, and that we could have this given back to us. We should put it into our body and then come back. That is how the instructions were given.

As soon as the rapid opening drum beats started, I saw the colours green and gold. I thought: "I do know a beautiful place in nature which has these two colours, but where is it?" I found myself descending into the arbour of the Sun Moon dance ceremony where the radiating golden tracks of the dancers are in contrast to the green spaces between. I was standing looking at the dance Tree. A bird landed on the top of the Tree. I wondered: "Is it an eagle?" I felt awed by this possibility, but it seemed rather smaller than an eagle. I called it down. It flew down onto my right wrist. It was a white blackbird with a yellow beak.

The drumming changed to begin the journey. The white blackbird flew violently at my right eye and tore it out. I was completely shocked. I thought: "Oh-aaah, what's going on? I want my eye back." It seemed unlikely that I would get it. I demanded it. There was no response. Then I said to the bird: "Well, you can have that eye as a gift." Immediately the bird flew away and I thought: "But that was the Being I was going to exchange gifts with and it has just flown off with my eye."

I turned to look at the dance Tree again. It was the most enormous White Eagle. All around me, the white feathers were close: I wasn't standing on the ground looking up, I was standing in the eye socket of the Eagle, the right eye was missing and the inner recesses of the eye socket were brown. Again totally shocked by this situation, I wondered what to do and I thought: "This eye socket is actually somewhat like a cave and we are supposed to be journeying into the lower world so, I will walk in." I walked in; it was the entrance to an underworld. I stood there and I worried: "But I haven't got an animal to travel with me." The deep voice of the Eagle spoke to me and said: "As long as you are within my body you are travelling with me, so, travel without fear."

The spinal column was a golden ladder and I began to descend. I climbed down, down, down into the body. Soon I found myself looking horizontally into the liver. I entered the liver. Integrated now into the Eagle's body I began to feel the journey taking place in my own body. I entered the gall bladder and words came to me: 'the bitter sea.' A black boat was stationed by the shore and a great, flat, tide-less expanse of dark ocean stretched away. I stepped into the black boat and it began to move out across the inky water.

I noticed a tall black bird standing ahead of me at the prow. Its wings were so tightly folded against its body that it looked as if it never used them. I wondered why a bird would be a ferryman of the underworld. I called it to me. It came to my left wrist and I said: "Look, I can see by your yellow legs and feet that you are a hunting bird. You are a hawk. Go, fly for me and bring me a present." The bird flew away and I was left alone in the boat. I asked myself: "Was that a good idea? Did I just send the power animal away? Am I afraid?" But I remembered the words of the Eagle. I was within the Eagle therefore I was not afraid.

The boat moved on across the black waters; it had no sails, no oars, no motor, no rudder, no crew, and yet it travelled purposefully over the calm and barren waste of the bitter sea. Suddenly, without warning, it spun round, one and a half turns, and I found myself in a different world. This world was very thin horizontally. There was only a narrow gap between the floor and the ceiling. There were some energies here that were like silk, that is the nearest I can describe them. They crackled and they felt like silk, they moved in long formations made of many fibres that made them seem to be like silk scarves, some were silver and some were gold. They entered my body through my navel centre, spiralling down as if they were being pulled by a whirlpool, slowly coiling themselves up as they entered into my body in that way.

Once inside me the scarves began to stretch themselves throughout my body and make me aware of all my body. The fibres ran down my legs, they ran in my arms, they ran everywhere, and I began to get a different sense of my body, which was not a thing composed of arms and legs, it was a thing composed of hundreds and thousands upon thousands of these filaments. It became apparent to me that the thing that I had lost was the knowledge of the nature of my body. As I grew older, this is what had disappeared, or been taken away from me, or I had no longer been able to connect to. I lay now in this horizontal layer of existence and began to stretch the fibres with my will, began to go even further into every nook and cranny. I was reminded of coral, when the polyps with all those little hairs come out and flick around in the water and can be withdrawn and disappear again into the hard coral case. I ran my fibres everywhere in this horizontal world and became aware of everything and knew that I could know everything that was there. Everything that was there was composed of light of various colours, green and pink and blue and gold. Everything was transparent in form and the fibres of my being could touch everything.

At this point, I paused, and I returned to the beginning of the journey and travelled it again, more intensely. I didn't ask myself why the bird took my eye. I didn't ask myself whether the socket of the eagle's eye was a cave. I didn't have to try to think at what place I had arrived and so everything happened more intensely and with more impact on my body. I came back to the same place. I wondered what would happen next.

I began to look at the fact that this world that I was in was not very deep but extended vastly horizontally. I looked up and I could see that the bitter sea was above this world and above that were all the other layers of my being. I drew all the filaments back from the horizontal world and gathered them into my navel centre. Then, in one movement, I pushed them out. As they shot up vertically through the layers of my being they disconnected all the connections, which held that thing together as something real, it didn't disappear but its restricting cohesion was lost. The bunch of fibres, which left my navel centre packed close together, spread out as they rose higher, spread out into what was like a tree made of fibres of light.

I was looking at this tree when the black bird landed high up in the branches. I called to it: "Come down. What have you brought me?" It had brought me a silver ring with a design engraved upon it. I put the ring on the third finger of my right hand. I was trying to work out what the design might be when I began to get annoyed with the bird. I don't know for what reason, but it had gone back to its original non-flying form. I took hold of it with my left hand. I felt how the hard feathers on its wings were compacted and how they seemed stuck to its body. I pushed it into my body, to the right of my heart, immediately everything felt extremely bad. I didn't like to have this strangely static bird inside me and I didn't like the ring. I pulled the bird out and threw it away. I took off the ring and I threw the ring away.

I looked again at my great luminous tree body and I wondered what to do with it. I opened it out so that there was a big space in the centre of all the fibres, thinking: "I could make something in here that makes things. That would be interesting." But I didn't do it.

Then a vision of the Eagle's face came to me; one of the eyes was missing. I said to myself: "I can make the eye of the Eagle. I can give the Eagle back its eye." As I made this eye, I became it. Maybe it took all the fibres that I had, or maybe I got so absorbed in the task that I put all of myself into it. The eye of the Eagle was back in the socket and perfect. I was just beginning to think that, as I was now an eye, I could look out and see what the Eagle saw when the drumming changed. The journey was over.

The journey was a very absorbing experience. I feel that the gift that I received was the return of my body awareness. And the gift that I gave? Reluctantly I gave my eye to the small and spiteful bird at the beginning of the journey, and, at the end, I gave myself, my eye, to the Great Bird who protected me and let me travel within it. Thank you, Eagle.

And the black wooden bird? There was a lot more work to be done to solve that mystery.

> Taking a Trip to the Middle World
> Go to an island. Meet your animal.
> Go through a mist, see what happens.

29. The Green Marsh

When it came to the time to make the middle world journey, I felt pretty shattered. I didn't want to journey to some deep place and bring back some precious piece of personal experience to have it obliterated by the, hah, shamanic insensitivity of this particular group.

I got ready to set off. I was standing on the shore looking at the island and I felt depressed. The whole of the day had depressed me because I felt that some people on the course were intimidated by the energy, which was running high. Afraid of the stream of power, as well as being envious of those who embraced it, they set out to destroy the vibe in an attempt to bring the situation under their rational control. I felt very depressed. I looked at the island and I thought: "I'll just swim there because I don't know how much effort I can make." I also wanted to make it difficult for myself, to hold myself up, some strange attempt to enter the group dynamic, I guess. With great reluctance, I waded in and, reaching deeper water, readying myself to swim I stretched my arms out in front of me. A smiling dolphin joined me, nudging me to play, and we played together in the water. It was extremely pleasant and enjoyable, and I just wanted to do that.

I just wanted to stay there and do that, which for a while I did, but then I knew that the journey was to go on and I climbed out of the water onto the stony beach. I suggested to the grey dolphin that, if it would swim round to the far side of the island, maybe I would be able to join it later, but it came out of the water with me and became the grey horse of the Ancient Grandfather. I was very glad to see this beautiful calm horse and I said: "Let's walk into the mist together." We did walk in together and in the mist we dissolved, our bodies dissolved, our personalities dissolved, and we became like swirling, drifting banks of cloud. In this form we began to play again; it was delightful to be so formless and so simple in our structure, so homogenous and yet insubstantial. To twist and turn and circle and spiral together, this was a kind of ecstasy. After a while I thought: "Oh, how tempting it is to stay here and do this, but I must travel on. It will not be acceptable that I got lost in the mist, or rather, that I refused to leave it. This is not an acceptable journey to bring back." I stepped out of the mist.

I was on my own and it was very difficult to formulate what I had walked into, but it was all bright green and also very wet. I decided that I had walked into an enormous marsh. I stood in this bright green, mossy, boggy environment and looked around. The air was very, very clear and I could see that this bog stretched for miles and miles, as far as the eye could see. Some kind of a wispy cloud form had come, maybe from the fog bank behind me, and was now apparent in front of me. It was a Will-o'-the-Wisp and it sighed: "Travel with me." The trouble bees (it sounds like this on the audio tape; the words are incomprehensible. Oh, it must be 'drum beats') started to say: "Come foll-ow us, come foll-ow us, come foll-ow us," as if, I don't know, as if some insubstantial formless spirits were calling. I, I looked for the Coyote to help me in this situation, but he said he didn't want to come on this journey. He said he was aware of what was happening, but he didn't want to travel today. So I ignored the trouble bees and stood there surveying the landscape.

Eventually, perhaps hearing my silent cries for help, the Owl came flying towards me. Unblinking, it observed me. I did not want to assume the owl body and I said: "Well, pick me up and fly with me." The Owl was not interested in carrying a lump like me and gave me to understand that I was perfectly capable of flying out of the swamp myself. But I just couldn't summon the impetus. I looked across the endless moss; it was far too far. I certainly did not want to wade through it either. That's right! The Owl said to me: "Look at your feet." I looked, and I did see my naked feet, but they were not in the place where I was standing. If you understand me, my feet were sunken in the bog and I could not see them, I simply saw my feet, as feet, and wondered what the Owl meant, something about my placement?

Eventually I got so fed up that I found the energy to levitate myself out of that morass. This done, I lay on my back horizontally in the open air, about six feet above the surface of the bog. I slipped into a trance-like space of, um, dark, um, lack of stimulus, I would say. This was a relief. I lay in that space, in a particular mental state that had no visual pictures and was without effort, for quite some time.

I heard an aircraft coming from the right. The noise got louder and louder. It flew so low over the top of the seminar building, and the room vibrated so much, that I thought it was soon going to crash. I was afraid of that sound. I clung to it, convinced that at any minute I was going to hear the impact of the crash. I got as far as imagining everybody in the room sitting up in shock at the explosion. That was a shattering scenario: the white faces experiencing the shock of the totally unexpected. Of course, it didn't crash and this distraction created a different mental space inside my brain and things began to happen where before there had only been emptiness.

I felt the spirits come and touch parts of me, what parts they were I was unable to articulate, and they changed them. In among all this the Owl returned. I perceived very clearly the body of the Owl. That body is also the tree and that is also me, the three of us are one.

After that, the drumming changed and the journey was over. The journey was such an incomprehensible mess at that stage that I began to review the fragile and disjointed contents to try and shape the pieces into something comprehensible. I had suffered from inertia at the beginning, not wanting to take a journey and have the experience disempowered by sharing it with the seminar group, and this reluctance had continued. I began to suspect something: "Where do these journeys come from and who are they for?" "In what sense are they my own and in what sense do they belong to the group?" I began to wonder about that dark space. What was happening there? That is what I wondered.

Travelling to the Upper World
Travel up a mountain with your animal.
Rise up through clouds. Go for it!

30. Through the Spirit Lodge

As we got ready to take this journey, I knew that I was going to visit the Ancestors. The drumming began and I called to the Buffalo. I stood next to the big brown and black body of the buffalo, our shoulders touched. We were standing here, in this world. Up in the sky was a great circular hole, which was held open by the horns of the buffalo, a hole through which the Ancestors entered and exited. The Buffalo and I walked together, we rose up together, we went through this hole, and we stood together on the Great Plains. The view was endless, endless beauty, endless calm beauty. I stood there with the Buffalo and I took hold of his left horn, because I was standing, always, on his left-hand side.

I looked again into the Great Plain and I saw a small buffalo skin lodge standing there some long distance away. I knew this was the buffalo spirit lodge, I thought to myself: "I have done this before. I can go straight there." I went straight there. I went straight inside. I thought: "I have done this before. I know how to go out of this lodge." I went up through the smoke hole and that is when I went through the cloud barrier.

Above me I saw the panorama of the night sky and a voice said to me: "Find your Star." I went. If I wanted to describe the direction, up, ahead and left of centre; that is where it would be. I travelled to this star. I knew that I was travelling to see the Star Maiden who came to see me once and I lost ninety per cent of the memory of her visit, but she had come to the Earth to visit me in a meditation and now I would go to visit her. I arrived at the star and I entered in; it was composed of crystalline colours, which were the essence of the beautiful Being, who, as I entered, entered me and especially entered me in the area below my heart, all the energy centres there.

I felt the Ancestors arriving, coming in feeling into my body. They were a great circular space that tingled on all the edges of my awareness, especially on the lower left-hand edge. This was the place where the Star Maiden came into my perception. When a certain point was reached, I looked more closely at the crystalline colours of light that composed the ancestral place. There was pink. I allowed the pink to enter my being and move in me. The same thing happened again and the colour was mauve, then green and then blue. The sensation of the blue was very different. It seemed possible to me that the whole journey could concentrate in the blue and that would be where my purpose was. Golden-yellow was the last colour of the light to enter and I began to line them up in my body. I lined them up. I thought I would return to the Earth with the colours in this order: first pink, then mauve, green next, blue and, finally, golden-yellow. I would come to the Earth like a shooting star with these colours trailing.

But it was not the time in the journey to do that. I looked back down at the Great Plains and I saw the tiny spirit lodge standing there. I spoke to the Star Maiden: "That place, when I am in it why do I get pestered and battered by all those spirit energies and why is it so confusing?" I looked down again from this place beyond and the lodge appeared to me as a beehive full of bees. That was an entirely appropriate image of the business of that place. Then I saw the honey in the hive and I seemed to understand that without the spirit lodge there would be no golden light perceivable below. I saw the black and yellow bees and I connected the energies of the spirit lodge with the yellow and black colours that make the day and night, the two lights, the duality that makes our world.

As I looked at the beehive, I heard: "In this way you can" followed by three words, I think they were 'feel, sense and be'. I know that 'be' was the last of the three words because it was a pun on the Bees and I knew I wouldn't forget that word. Yes, I am pretty sure that the words were 'sense, feel and be', so the sentence was: "In this way you can sense, feel and be."

Then I returned to the essence of the Star Maiden, the Star Maiden who I am deeply in love with, who brings a certain ecstasy to my psyche that is available nowhere else, and I said to her: "Press farther into my being. Push farther into my awareness." Because, until now, this great circle of ancestral awareness had only been in my lower centres. She answered my request; the crystalline colours began to push further up my body and they travelled up through my heart centre and into my brain. Somewhere deep in my brain in the back lobes on the right-hand side they came to a halt, or a barrier, or a blockage, or a density, or a, um, what would I call it? an obfuscation. This was black and, in the first moment, I was shocked to find the colour black here where the Star Maiden had penetrated with the light. Then I remembered: "But I like black. In fact, I love black, and I love to travel in the black light, and the black light teaches me many things." But there was some sense in which the essence of the Star Maiden and this blackness in my brain were not compatible.

Yes, the light found this black place and I thought: "Do I need help in this place?" As I looked, purple light came, Joseph comes with purple light, and that was what was needed in this dark place. The darkness needed to be fused with the purple light in order for something to happen. In order for the next thing to happen? I don't know but the black and the purple met together, and they mixed. As that happened my head and then my body began to stretch in a great arc. They stretched and bowed and travelled down towards the Great Plains, and I felt the black and purple lights enter first into the smoke hole of the buffalo skin lodge. They entered in and the whole of my being stretched out behind me. My feet were still attached to the star and the colours radiated back from my head towards it: the purple, then the black, followed by the yellow, the blue, the green, the mauve and, finally, the pink, closest to the star.

Yes, I stretched down like a night-bow in the sky, and then I was within the buffalo lodge. The whole lodge collapsed and fell flat as if it was a skin lying on the ground. Now this, maybe, was something that I thought might have been a good idea to get rid of all that pesky astral stuff. But, as soon as the skin was lying flat on the ground, I realized that all connection between the worlds above and below was lost. I decided to reconstruct the lodge. I stood up inside it, in this way raising the roof and re-forming it into a mound shape. While I was doing that, the Buffalo came in physical form to collect me. We came back through the great hole in the sky. We stood again, here on the Earth, together.

I looked at my solar plexus; it was green and grass was growing there. I lay down on my back and I said to the Buffalo: "Eat. Eat the grass. Be nourished." The tongue of the Buffalo, which was quite purple, came and wrapped itself around the grass and pulled it. For the last few moments of the journey I watched the Buffalo eating the grass, eating the grass right here on this plain, and that was something wonderful.

Before the journey started, I knew that there would be agony somewhere. I knew that there would. I was completely delighted that I never found it during the drumming; the entire journey was blissful, heavenly, ecstatic. But I did find agony when I came out of the trance state, agony, yes, absolute agony, a sense of loss, a terrible, terrible, sense of loss. Although the world looked very pleasant, and the tree through the window was very beautiful, and the people in the room were all friendly, I felt an intense longing that made me cry for a minute or two. Then it diminished away.

When I knew that agony would at some point come, I also knew that I would never deprive myself of the ecstasy, which was to be found way out there, because of some minor little agony that I might suffer when I came back. It doesn't feel quite so minor now!

The fact that my feet remained with the Star Maiden shines a new light on the journey yesterday when the Owl said: "Look at your feet." I looked and, despite my situation, my feet were not sunk out of sight in the bog, I saw my naked feet. Today, as I lay waiting, shoes off, for the session to begin, several people who passed me tickled my feet so they must have been drawn to touch them to bring my attention to them. My feet? My feet dwell in the Star.

TEN

Flying Free

Entering the Black Buffalo

The Peace Being

The Healing Quest
Ask the power animal
for advice, help or a gift.

31. Flying Free

My interior space was pitch dark. It was pitch dark as Alexander spoke his introduction to the power animals. It was pitch dark as the drumming began. I travelled down a pitch dark tunnel and I came into the presence of a Thunder Being, very, very hazy and difficult to formulate, full of black and yellow vortices. Way below in the intense darkness I could see that there was something for me. I went down.

It was in my abdomen that this something was waiting. I saw slanting green lines on either side supporting between them a milky-white diamond-shape. I looked at it for a long time, wondering what it was, and eventually I decided to touch it. As I picked it up, I recognised it from a journey long ago where my ovaries had become my eyes but now there was more: the green plant-like ovaries were there, sure, on either side, but the diamond-shaped stone in the centre was new, and the completed image was a flowering of my ovaries and my womb. As I lifted it up I noticed with excitement that I could put it into any energy centre, but actually I never got farther than placing it in one centre, the eye centre, because immediately I did that I travelled forwards at high speed straight into the translucent stone.

I began to see the vast expanse of the Great Plains below me. The Great Plain was utterly empty and I felt an impelling need to get to the spirit lodge. I saw it in the distance and I got there. I am not exactly sure how I went in, except that my entry was fast and effective. Today the lodge was low with a vast diameter, the roof was flat, and it was full of spirits. I joined the many other Beings that were circling below the ceiling. The colour of the swirling spirits was mainly brown, but there were also black ones and yellow too, I myself was yellow, and grey ones, a very small number of them were grey. They all moved in the same direction and an intricate swirling design was created by the flowing colours.

A flap in the roof of the lodge flew open, and we all went out in a great rush. As we came out our colours became lights, changing to many shades of pink and blue. It was wonderful to fly freely in the blue sky. We circled and mingled there for some time, like birds preparing for migration; then the shout went up: "Let's go to the Great Spirit!" and we flew upwards towards the place where the Great Spirit was to be found.

We reached the boundary and we went through a barrier into the presence of an enormous She-Bear. Her immense body was like one of those rocks called geodes, that, when broken open, are found to be hollow inside and full of crystal structures hidden, until then, by the rough brown exterior. She was pink within and contained a pink crystal world. Well, it was beautiful to be there and I drifted in the great body of the Bear looking at the translucent crystal formations. I thought about the seminar group. I thought: "Some people expect me to travel with the Coyotes. Where are the Coyotes?" A stern voice spoke: "Don't destroy Beauty with your wild dreams."

As I listened, I knew I had reached the place where I could receive the gift of my healing power. I knew that this sentence was a healing gift, so I tried hard for some time to make sure that I remembered the exact words, knowing how these things can vanish utterly and how I could be left with only the memory that some certain words were spoken. The way I remembered it was the reverse of the way I remember my car number plate, which I do by making a mnemonic sentence. This time I reduced the sentence to its initials, D D B and then, W Y W D: "D-on't D-estroy B-eauty W-ith Y-our W-ild D-reams." Now, don't ask me how that made me able to remember it, but it did, and those letters served me well.

After hearing the sentence and making the memory catcher for it, I allowed that sentence to do something to me. What it did to me was that it asked me to fall, to drop my thoughts about what was going on, to drop even my picture-making ability. Oh, this was extremely hard. All the while I was thinking: "I am not achieving it. I can't do it. I am not achieving it ......" when suddenly I did find myself in a completely other place.

The spirits said: "Step out. Step out of your body." I did, and I saw my body lying there. I also saw the shadow of what was rising out of the many bodies lying there. It was a looming, chunky, long armed, square bodied shadow. I couldn't see hands or feet, but I could see big arms and legs, a neckless head and a large rectangular body. Now there were many people in this cave, but there was only one reflection there.

It was then I noticed that the drum beat was coming from the very centre of our group. I really believed that Alexander had moved from the periphery to the centre. This was impossible because people were lying all around the medicine altar, which was placed in the middle, but still the sound of the drum was coming from the centre. How strange to be suddenly out of that cave and in this world of consciousness but was it quite this world? As I wondered, about the locations of and the boundaries between the various worlds, my journey returned to the cave.

At the sound of the drum, the flame from the central fire pulsed and the shadow on the wall moved, so the figure danced when the vibration of the drum beat hit the source of the light and made the light flicker. I was busy watching this when a request, addressed to unknown listeners, formulated itself in my mind and I asked them: "May I do some work now, please?" Within two drum beats, the journey had finished and Alexander was drumming us back. Wow! I rooted into that space and there was NO way I was coming back. "NO, I will stay here! NO, I will NOT leave this behind." Then, the voice of the forward motion of my life in this world, I suppose, said: "This is the moment to call the Coyotes." And I called them.

They came and they dragged me, kicking and screaming, out of that cave. They made themselves into a zebra crossing and they said: "Walk across the lines." The zebra crossing, far from crossing a road, became a road itself, and they kept saying to me: "Walk across the lines, black to yellow, black to yellow, black to yellow."

My impulse was to veer off to the right and start walking up one of the lines, one colour or the other, and not to walk across them, but I listened to them and I walked a torturous winding path.

Then I worried: "This isn't going back through the journey." I cast a glance to the right and I saw the palace of the Crystal Bear. I felt confident then. They brought me back through the place where the Bear resided, into the blue sky and into the spirit lodge. In the lodge, I felt the agony of not living in a continuous state of awareness in the spirit place. Anyway, I came back through that and came back here. I hope I remembered to thank the Coyotes for bringing me back, but I have a feeling that I may have forgotten and so I thank them now.

<u>Journey to the Inner Temple</u>
Find inner healing and healing power.

32. Entering the Black Buffalo

The music started and I entered the journeying consciousness. Maybe I was a little too optimistic at the beginning of this journey. I had the idea that if I pushed to make something happen, it would happen and that is how I set off. But everything I tried to do, everything I tried to move and every time I tried to travel, nothing happened.

I began to be of the opinion that, by the intrusion of my desires, I was going to be going absolutely nowhere. I let go a bit and I began to travel in the darkness, travelling through a night sky full of silver light, going back to the experience last night of seeing the aurora borealis and travelling onwards. Seeing and travelling into a black pyramid and beginning to consider the impression I have of a life spent in the cool, dark temple in Khemet. I accepted the darkness, accepted the movement, and began to travel through a series of ancient buildings, one of which had silver light entering through a hole in the ceiling. But nothing happened in these places and I continued to travel on.

I had become quite resigned to the fact that I would simply travel in the darkness, seeing the occasional temple and sanctuary, till the end of the music, when I saw ahead of me the head of the Black Buffalo. I said: "I know you. I have seen you before." When I had first seen the Black Buffalo, it was tiny, dense, invertedly energetic; its whole body so tightly curled up on itself that it was condensed into a dark ball. Now only the head was hanging there in the black space, much larger than myself. I travelled slowly towards it, observing the curly, metallically coloured black coat, the very broad, flat forehead and the wide spreading horns. In the very centre of the forehead was a golden hole from which issued forth golden light. I put my solar plexus to that golden hole. The image was graphic. The sensation was powerful. Through that hole I went, into the space that is within that Black Buffalo Being.

A surprise awaited me. It was a very peculiar place in there. It was dark, but it was not black, the space was fizzing with whiteness. I felt my awareness of my shape change. I began to lose my body contours and to become, I presumed, the shape of the buffalo, but it was a round contour-less shape that I became and after that absolutely nothing changed. There was a feeling of intense density and pressure and I only had my awareness left. I had nothing else; the awareness of being fizzing dark matter filled my consciousness. The sensation was not painful, it was not threatening. It was ......, I'd like to use the word 'ghastly'. It was a very difficult place to be in because there was nothing to be experienced there except density and pressure.

I searched through my experience for something similar. The only thing it reminded me of was when I was a child, sometimes when I lay in bed at night, my head used to feel very huge. The childhood sensation that went with that was like crunching cotton wool in your hand, but the sensation on this journey was like a pressing weight, an immobile pushing-ness, a kind of suffocation. It did not take my breath; I seemed not to breathe. I distinctly did not like being in there, and, although the sensation was extraordinary and I was certainly questioning what on earth kind of a place it was, I would have very much liked to get out of it, but I couldn't see how that was possible. I seemed to have lost my body and to have lost the ability to move. I noticed that panic was an option, and I determined to stay calm.

Into the darkness I called very quietly: "Grandfather?" hoping that he would hear and help me. When I called the pressure and the sensation that was so strange began to diminish at once and the strange darkness began to become pure black light. With relief, I knew that the Grandfather would take me out of there, but, as I felt the place diminish, I became aware that somehow this outcome was disappointing. The Grandfather would never make me suffer when I could not stand it, but I felt a sense of defeat in coming out and I chose to go back.

I went back. It was exactly as it had been and it became very clear to me that I had to surrender in that place because there was nowhere else to go and nothing else to do. I did surrender and something broke inside me. Something around the level of my solar plexus seemed to be laid upon a block there and broken in half, like a piece of brittle metal. It snapped and tears rolled out of my eyes. It was a terrible moment because that was the end: that was it.

Very shortly after this catastrophic self-sacrificial moment for nothing, that strange state began to diminish and I came back to my body lying flat on its back in the seminar room. Yes, tears were falling out of my eyes and running into my ears quite fast. I lay looking at the shadow of the centre light on the ceiling. Due to the candle burning on the medicine altar directly underneath, there was a black shadow cast on the ceiling with a white centre and another black circle in the centre of that. This made a kind of eye. I looked at it for a long time, wondering if it would take me on another journey, but it did not, and, quite frankly, I was happy just to be back lying there in a familiar room.

I did not think I would journey further, but then the CD jammed and I was aware that Alexander got up to fix it. When he came back, his presence came back with him and I was aware of him lying there. This changed the dynamic and I was able to go to a small, round, white pillared temple perched on a pinnacle of rock overlooking a sparkling blue sea far below. In the centre of this small temple, there was a golden sphere of light energy into which I entered. The golden light was beautiful and nurturing. Then I went into a warm blue light and a dolphin came and played with me. The most fun thing we did together was being suspended among the bubbles of air that rose from below in a continuous stream. That was a pleasant sensation and the journey came to an end. This final section seemed like a treat for me and I certainly enjoyed it.

I don't know what the speckled place was. I did wonder if it was the Void. I wouldn't like to decide on that. Later on I thought that Black Buffalo might have been the Minotaur at the centre of the labyrinth, but I wouldn't like to decide on that either. All I know is that the Grandfather would have taken me out of that state had I persisted in my request and this proves to me that nothing is done by compulsion in the spirit world. It is all done by choice, and it is very possible that I made the right choice there, to go back, and that pleased the Grandfather. But he would not have been displeased with me if I had come out; I would have been displeased with myself.

Yes, I would have preferred to forget this journey and, instead of going away to record it, I talked to Alexander in the seminar room till late at night (not about the journey, no way), but it has not left my mind, as I knew it wouldn't. The intensity of the feeling I had there has diminished and I have slightly lost exactly what I did give up down there. So that's it: that was my journey to my inner temple. Hah!

Next Steps Journey
Use your imagination!

33. The Peace Being

As soon as the journey started everything went black and I saw the head of the Black Buffalo, which was the Apis Bull, which was the Minotaur, which, as it turned out, was the bull-leapers' Bull from Knossos. The horns of this bull Buffalo Being were golden, gilded, perhaps, for a ceremony; I jumped, leaping through the space between them, using my arms to push me and to give me the impetus to fly.

I travelled upwards into an intense sensation of the Coyote. "Hello, beautiful Coyote, I feel your physical body. I feel your loving presence. I feel the warmth and the heat and the goodness of our connection." We began to travel through space, rolling, rolling together, spiralling, and driving onwards through space, travelling towards the boundaries of the planetary atmosphere. This was ecstasy.

I looked down and I saw streams of yellow and black light exiting my feet like spent fuel from a rocket ship; I realized that the Coyotes were burning up and disappearing in the energy of this journey. My euphoria vanished and I was overcome with grief: I was losing them.

We reached the limits of the atmosphere and they were no longer able to be there. I stood alone at the barrier between this world and something else, seeing a circular hole. The thinnest membrane exists between this world and the next and the hole in it is surrounded by a silver rim, which keeps the way open. A voice said to me: "Step through." But I found myself unable to take that step. Instead, I spent a long time minutely examining the silver rim, which is very thin, very fine, and hard and strong as steel. I was grieving over the loss of my power animals. My desolation was intense. I did not want to go on.

I knew I needed to go through the hole, but I could not step, I could not make my feet move, so I led with my head and I tipped off that place and into space. There was no sensation of falling; I drifted, looking but seeing nothing, looking and looking and seeing nothing, feeling rather despairing and still feeling the loss of the beauty and the pictures of the Coyotes and the picture-full world that they live in.

I needed help. I saw Joseph standing in the space there. He was motionless and yet he directed my attention. Looking past him, I saw the form of something like a range of high mountains. I knew that these mountains were the Peace Beings. I tried hard to see them more clearly, hoping to be able to understand what the vision of World Peace is and how it can possibly come about. Try as I might, I couldn't see any more.

One Being stepped forward from the rest of that vast mountain range and that Being gave me a gift of green light. I looked at the green light and I felt myself moving somewhat slightly back towards this place. The green light went golden. I began to think of the golden light body that Alexander suggests we might visualize as we channel healing and I asked: "Why can I not visualize the golden light body when I am working on people in this seminar learning spiritual healing? Why do I see a black body, somewhat the shape of the physical body, lying on the ground, a long, thin oval; and, above it, why do I see that haze of black with goldenness inherent in it, looking somewhat like tarnished ancient bronze; and why do I see, outside of that, a thin band of clear light, which has perhaps a vaguely green hue to it; and, outside of that, why do I see another band of black; and, beyond that, why do I see that there is the possibility of the golden light body, which is not actually there? Why do I see this? And why can I not see the golden light body?" I called out to the Peace Spirits: "Why is it like this?" I did not get an answer, but I did have that very graphic image of what I do see.

I was drifting, thinking of this question. I must have drifted near to the hole because the paw of the Coyote came in and he grabbed me. He hooked me, pulled me out through the hole and embraced me fervently. I felt the love come through the thick golden coat of the Coyote and envelop me in a deep and loving embrace. I was so happy that he was still around to love me in that way.

Within two seconds, the music was fading and Alexander was asking us to return. Lying waiting for the group sharing to begin I began to travel back through the journey. I looked at the silver rimmed hole and I saw that the Peace Being, the one who had stepped forward to give me the light, had come to the portal there and was going to come through. I was shocked. When I was through on the other side I was overwhelmed, feeling that if I could not clearly see the Peace Beings then I would not be able to bring anything back into the world that could help to manifest the vision here, but this Peace Being had come to the portal and was coming through. I called out and I said: "I am sorry. I am sorry to diminish you." As I said this I hit a whole new wave of grief.

The Peace Being came through the hole and, as it came through, it transformed and became a pink crystal flower. I saw a Rose, a Rose made of rose quartz crystal so that it was strong, long lasting and beautiful. The Peace Being had transformed itself, come here and become that beautiful thing.

I was completely overcome; I wept and tears were streaming out of my eyes. I did think this morning that if I meditated with the Grandfather, the pain of this journey would diminish, and, certainly, it has because I have been able to put it on the tape without being overcome by emotion. But yesterday, right to the evening, I only had to think of two things, the loss of the Coyote on the way out and the diminishment of the Peace Being on the way in, to feel those emotions well up inside me and the tears begin to come.

So that is my pain, but, to my joy, the Coyote is indestructible and a Peace Being has come here.

Abouts

About the Author

Throughout my life, I have slowly moved north. I was born and grew up on a farm in Suffolk, England, moved north to University in my twenties and stayed on in North Yorkshire running a business until, in my fifties, I moved to Morayshire in Scotland where I still live and write my books.

As a child I was a prolific dreamer and would tell my dreams every morning at breakfast. My mother was so worried that she wanted me to see a psychiatrist, but my father replied emphatically: "No child of mine is going to a trick-cyclist."

And so I was spared but, somewhere along the way, I stopped sharing my dreams so readily. Nevertheless, I always felt connected to a greater something and would seek confirmation from the natural world that I was still in harmony with that mysterious unknown.

Sometime in my forties, my partner at that time challenged me, saying I could not prove anything and that the 'spiritual' did not exist. Maybe he was right, certainly I could not prove anything, and I decided to live like he did; I decided to try living in a world where there was no enveloping mystery.

I lived in that world for so long that I forgot it was an experiment until one overwhelming day I noticed that I had completely lost my sense of connection. I called for help. The cry was in my mind, I saw it resonate through many layers of being which, until that moment, I had not known anything about, and swiftly back came Help into the world of every day.

That Help was so helpful to me that, after five years of travelling in those unknown realms, I decided to write some books about aspects of my journeys that might inspire others to explore the vastness of their personal consciousness.

And that is why I think it is important to write books.

About this Book

Finding a Teacher was not the first of all the helpful things that came to me, but it was the most important and so, in order to honour our connection, I chose to publish first this book of trance journeys taken under his guidance.

Quite early in my life I had come to the conclusion that there were no gurus any more; that the challenge in this Age was for each person to choose to live morally and to find their individual way through the labyrinth with integrity. I was not looking for a Teacher, but I was looking.

I had some experience of the Theosophical Society earlier in my life and joined the local group. They met in the Friends' Meeting House, on the notice board I saw that there was a spiritual healing group meeting there on the same night every week. I was interested and I soon switched groups. A weekend seminar was imminent; the group's organiser would run it with a friend. Some things happened that weekend which convinced me that the 'friend' was part of the Help coming my way and I wrote to ask him if I could become his student. He wrote back: "The signs are right. Yes."

Now I know why it helps to have a living Teacher when you wish to go beyond the world of everyday. They teach you rules of journeying: how to leave, and how to return safely with memory of the experience. And then there is the special bond of Love, which keeps the student anchored in the world of daily life.

My Teacher gave me many gifts, often without a word passing between us. The greatest gift was that when I glanced at him for approval he was always looking the other way and so I was given the opportunity to take full responsibility for my experiences, opinions and actions: it was a liberation.

For me, the stories in this book demonstrate how much help is to be found through altered state journeying and other such techniques that empower the individual to experience their selves (I use 'their selves' advisedly).

About the Travelling Technique

The journeys in this book were all taken during the course of various seminars led by my Teacher. He would give very specific instructions, telling us where we going to travel and what we should look for there, as specified in the text at the beginning of each story. He would remind us to meet a power animal who would be our guide and would bring us back safely. We should also endeavour to come back exactly the way that we went.

The journeys were generally taken to the regular beat of a hand drum. Rapid beats marked the beginning, allowing the travellers to prepare themselves, and rapid beats marked the end, instructing the travellers to return. Occasionally my Teacher would put on a CD of music he had chosen; on those occasions he would join us in travelling. A period of silence would follow to allow everyone to absorb their experience. After that there was always a sharing.

My method was to lie down flat on my back, close my eyes and relax. It would not take long before I no longer felt my physical body and the pictures would start. It was most important to be and to remain completely still, with the exception, of course, of the autonomous systems; any other movement would break the trance and also, very likely, erase the memory of the journey.

Bringing the memory back is one of the main challenges of altered state journeying. To fix the experiences in my memory I used the instruction to make sure to come back the way I went. If that was impossible, I relied on the power animal to carry the memory, and sometimes me, back.

All such journeys should be done under controlled conditions, within clearly defined parameters. This book is a testament to how empowering it can be to find a Teacher.

And why do I think this type of altered state work is important? It can give access to realms of consciousness where things that are dysfunctional or broken in our Being can be fixed.

Other Books by the Author

On Trees

Leaving my 'safe' house and walking alone in remote places, I battle with my personal problems. It is a battle that occupies the majority of my attention, but while I am engaged upon it natural forces come in to play with my consciousness.

This book contains colour photos of the places and the birds that feature in the text.

Being of Earth

Loving the Buffalo from before I can remember, I am happy to travel through all times and all spaces in their company. I follow their wanderings until we come to the present moment: a place where the future is Green.

Colour sketches are included in the text as an aid to visualization.

contents		page
ONE	1. Crashing through Fire	2
	2. Burnt Out	3
	3. The Metal Man	6
	4. Roads are Measured in Feet	10
TWO	5. Safe in the Sky	15
	6. Green Eyes	16
	7. Live Lightly	19
	8. The Fall	21
THREE	9. Flexible Boundaries	26
	10. The Four Beings	27
	11. Walking the Tight Rope	31
	12. Coyote Goes to Hollywood	35
FOUR	13. The Seven Jewels	41
	14. The Whole Secret	43
	15. Visiting the Celestial City	45
FIVE	16. Who Has the Power?	50
	17. The Art of Becoming	52
	18. In the Wood	55
	19. The Rocket Ship	59
SIX	20. Be content with the Blue	63
SEVEN	21. Taken by the Eagle	66
	22. The Many Grains of Sand	68
	23. The Tourist	72
	24. The Diamond Tip	76
EIGHT	25. Getting Up the Elephant's Nose	79
	26. The Ascending Spiral	83
	27. The Way to the Stars	86
NINE	28. In the Eagle's Body	89
	29. The Green Marsh	93
	30. Through the Spirit Lodge	96
TEN	31. Flying Free	101
	32. Entering the Black Buffalo	104
	33. The Peace Being	107
	About the Author	i
	About this book	ii
	About the Travelling Technique	iii
	Other Books by the Author	iv

www.ingramcontent.com/pod-product-compliance
Lightning Source LLC
Chambersburg PA
CBHW061801070526
44586CB00023B/2666